Dan Burritt

Jimmy Swaggart Ministries
P.O. Box 262550 | Baton Rouge, Louisiana 70826-2550 www.jsm.org

ISBN 979-8-992223-01-9
09-185 | COPYRIGHT © 2025 Jimmy Swaggart Ministries®
25 26 27 28 29 30 31 32 33 34 / Sheridan / 10 9 8 7 6 5 4 3 2 1

All rights reserved. Printed and bound in U.S.A.

All Scriptures are from the New King James Version, unless otherwise noted.

No part of this publication may be reproduced in any form or
by any means without the publisher's prior written permission.

DEDICATION

I wish to dedicate this book to the most special person in my life, my wife, Dorene. I thank the Lord for giving you to me more than forty years ago. You are the greatest help meet a man could ever ask for. Your faith has never wavered and has been an inspiration to me. Thank you, my honey, for your dedication to the ways of God, which have helped mold my life and keep me on track with the Lord. I love you more than words could ever express. You are the best mother and grandmother on the planet. We have our hands to the plow together, and we will not look back, in Jesus' name!

CONTENTS

Foreword 1
Preface...5
Acknowledgments..7
Chapter 1	The Sin Nature 9
Chapter 2	The Strength Of Sin Is The Law.............15
Chapter 3	Looking Unto Jesus.........................23
Chapter 4	Our Willpower Is Not Enough 29
Chapter 5	The Wretched Man Moment 39
Chapter 6	Deny Self And Die..........................51
Chapter 7	Obedience.................................59
Chapter 8	Separated To The Gospel 65
Chapter 9	Baptized Into Christ 73
Chapter 10	No Condemnation 87
Chapter 11	The Law Of The Spirit 95
Chapter 12	The Willful Sin 101
Chapter 13	Sanctified And Preserved Blameless........ 107
Chapter 14	Sanctified By Faith In Me 117
Chapter 15	The Message Of The Cross 125
Chapter 16	God's Wisdom, The Cross................. 139
Chapter 17	Jesus Christ And Him Crucified 147
Chapter 18	Positional Sanctification 157
Chapter 19	Progressive Sanctification 167
Chapter 20	How To Walk In The Spirit................ 177
Chapter 21	The Law: When, Why, And How? 191
Chapter 22	Sanctifying Rest.......................... 209
Chapter 23	Crucified With Christ 227
Chapter 24	Justification By Faith..................... 241
Chapter 25	God The Justifier 253
Chapter 26	Salvation Of The Sinner................... 263
Chapter 27	Baptized Into The Holy Spirit 273
Chapter 28	As You Have Received 285

FOREWORD

In 1995, I didn't know Dan Burritt, and he didn't know me. But the Lord would change all of that, and I'm so thankful He did. After being powerfully saved two years earlier, Dan, who owned and operated a bridge building business in upstate New York, finally gave in to his wife's persistence about attending one of our camp meetings here in Baton Rouge. So, in November of 1995, the Burritts came and brought with them their two young daughters. Dan later told how, on the first night of camp meeting, a Wednesday, he was just looking around, wondering, "What in the world is all this?" The next night, during praise and worship, he raised up one hand. On Friday night, both hands went up. Then, on Saturday night, he received the mighty baptism with the Holy Spirit, and his entire world changed. After that, I don't think he missed a single camp meeting.

It was just a couple years later that the Lord began revealing to me what He gave the apostle Paul so long ago—the message of the cross, which refers, in part, to sanctification and how to live for God. Dan got ahold of this great truth and, coupled with the call of God on his life, the result was him traveling to preach and teach in twenty-eight countries on five different continents. Along the way, he also put more than 860,000 copies of The Expositor's Study Bible into the hands of pastors and Christian workers around the world.

One of those places was a Bible college in Leyte, an island in the Philippines. After hearing Dan teach on the message of the cross for several years, the college changed its slogan to, "Without rice, or price, we will preach Christ and Him crucified."

Dan also spent time preaching in Nicaragua. In March of 2019, Dan was in Nicaragua for a pastors' conference and, while there, he was called and told, "President Ortega has opened up the Congress for you. He wants you to preach to the in-session Congress, inside the chambers." So Dan preached the gospel to their members of Congress and gave an altar call—all of it broadcasted over their government channel to the entirety of the country. Afterward, Dan gave every person in that chamber a copy of The Expositors' Study Bible. And it didn't end there, President Ortega then took Dan around to other government agencies, so that they, too, could hear the gospel message. Later, Dan's wife, Dorene, had the opportunity to pray with Rosario Ortega, the first lady and vice president of the country. She relayed to Dorene what a blessing it was when, some thirty years earlier, Frances and I were in Nicaragua for a crusade. The first lady said how that crusade changed the country and had brought peace and help in a time of war. I remember that crusade. It was held outdoors in Revolution Square. Thousands were there, maybe tens of thousands, and, at an extremely tense time in that country, the Spirit of God moved in a powerful way, and we believe many gave their hearts to Christ.

Also in Nicaragua, Dan traveled with others in a canoe loaded down with Bibles—a fourteen- hour ride one way on the Coco River—into remote jungle areas to preach the gospel and distribute Bibles to the Miskito Indians who live there.

You'll have to forgive my exuberance in relating to you some of the places that Dan Burritt reached with the gospel, but I've always had a heart for missions and a deep respect for God-called missionaries.

To fully appreciate what God is doing on the mission field, you really have to experience it for yourself. It's heartbreaking to see how much of the world lives with so little. These are not easy places to be. Frances and I still remember our visits to the foreign field—the high heat, the bugs, thick dust, the smells, food you sometimes can't stomach, the constant threat of disease. It's uncomfortable to be there. But in these places of raw poverty, there is also raw faith that responds to the preaching of the gospel.

Between missions trips, Dan would return to Baton Rouge and join me on *The Message of the Cross* and *A Study In The Word*. I thoroughly enjoyed hearing all he encountered in his work for God as a missionary evangelist. He and his lovely wife, Dorene, were also regulars on *Frances & Friends*. In April of 2019, they were on-air with Frances discussing the very real hardships of missionary life. "But we never complain," Dan said, "This is what we're called to do, and we're happy to do it.

And the reason we go is to teach the pastors justification by faith, sanctification by faith, the sin nature, how to live for God—and it's all contained in the Bible that we're able to give them."

Little did we know that fourteen months later, the Lord would call Dan Burritt home. By then I had known Dan for more than twenty years, so when they told me the news that he had passed away, it was like somebody had hit me, hard. Whenever we lose someone like that, someone of Dan's caliber, it's a tremendous loss for the kingdom of God. So why does God allow such things to happen? I can't answer that. What I do know is that God never makes a mistake; there is a reason for it, although most of the time the Lord does not choose to let us know what it is.

I miss Dan Burritt. He was a preacher of the cross unparalleled and a tremendous blessing to the work of God. He made the years that God gave him count, yes he did. In fact, just before the Lord called him home, Dan finished building one more bridge—the book you're holding in your hands—and it's for every believer who wants to cross over from the place of defeat to the place of victory in Christ Jesus. What you're about to read arches high above the great divide of religion, man-made systems, and self. It's about understanding sin and the sin nature in man. It's about experiencing justification and sanctification through faith in Christ and what He did for us on the cross. In other words, dear saint, it's about how to live for God, told in a way that only Dan could tell it.

—Evangelist Jimmy Swaggart

PREFACE

I never imagined I would write a book, but the Lord is always full of surprises. When I was first saved more than twenty-five years ago, I was so happy and full of faith. I was delivered from a miserable lifestyle full of sin, and all I wanted to do was make it to heaven. Within a short period of time, I found myself struggling with alcohol, and I became a miserable Christian. I was in church on Sunday, drinking on Monday, repenting on Tuesday, back in church on Wednesday, and drinking again on Thursday. This went on for several months. My pastor was right to tell me to stop drinking. However, he did not know what to tell me as far as *how* to stop drinking. How does a Christian get victory over a sin that so easily besets him?

Many ministers all over the world are preaching *what* to do, but they simply do not know *how* to do it. When the answer came, it was joy unspeakable and full of glory once again! It is so simple that it will bless your soul. This is something we must learn from the Word of God. I have written this book in plain language. You will not find big, five-thousand-dollar words or philosophical quips in this teaching.

As the Lord reveals this great truth, you will begin to learn how to live for God. This great truth is not something new; it is as old as the Bible itself. This truth can be found from Genesis to Revelation. It is the message of the cross. Understanding more about the cross of our Lord Jesus Christ will allow you to live the abundant life that Jesus promised. He did not promise sinless perfection, but He did promise victory over the devil, the flesh, the world, and sin. My prayer is that you will know how to live for God and also be able to share it with others in plain language. Glory to His name!

ACKNOWLEDGMENTS

First and foremost, I would like to give honor to my Lord and Savior Jesus Christ. He is my all in all and my everything. I cannot imagine my life without Him. From the day He found me, picked me up, and carried me, my life has been full of peace and joy. He is my redemption, my righteousness, and my sanctification. Thank You, Lord, for who You are and all that You have done in my life. I love You with all my heart.

I wish to thank my pastor, my teacher, and my friend, Brother Jimmy Swaggart. Thank you, Brother Swaggart, for your lifelong dedication to the work of God. You are a five-star general in God's army. The Lord has honored you by giving you the message of the cross to proclaim to the world for the end-times. The message of the cross that you teach has not only equipped me to write this book, but it has also changed my life, my family, and millions of other Christians around the globe. Hallelujah! The Lord is just getting started. One day in heaven, we will sing together praises to the Lamb.

Lastly, words cannot express my gratitude for the many, many hours that Amanda Arnold and Angela Arnold Girona offered as unto the Lord to edit this book. May God richly bless them and their families. Thank you, my sisters!

HOW TO LIVE FOR GOD

in plain language...

CHAPTER 1

THE SIN NATURE

CHAPTER ONE

THE SIN NATURE

The first step for a believer to understand how to live for God, is to know the difference between the acts of sin and the sin nature. Because of Adam's rebellion in the garden of Eden, we are all born with the sin nature and the acts of sin follow. Throughout this book, we will be discussing the sin nature that causes us to sin and how the Christian is to have victory over it.

The Greek word for sin, used many times in the book of Romans, is *hamartia*. It is a noun—a person, place, or thing. This is different from the verb tense for sin, *hamartano*, which is an action word for the acts of sin.

If you take two one-year-old children and put them together with only one toy, you will see the sin nature at work producing the acts of sin. They will fight, steal, and lie at only one year old. These young children are born with the sin nature, as are we, and that is why we sin. Some might say, "Now that I am saved, I no longer have a problem with sin."

But we all have the sin nature within us even after we are saved. However, the sin nature is not to control the believer.

> *"For sin* [the sin nature] *shall not have dominion over you, for you are not under law but under grace"* (Rom. 6:14).

The book of Romans was written to the believers that are saved by grace. So clearly, the sin nature is in us, but it must not dominate the Christian.

> *"So that as sin reigned in death, even so grace might reign through righteousness to eternal life through Jesus Christ our Lord"* (Rom. 5:21).

We have learned from the Word of God that the sin nature is in all of us. It was reigning in our lives before we came to Christ. When something reigns over us, it is our king, and we are subject to it. Before we are saved, the sin nature is our king. It was controlling our lives and leading us to death. But one glorious day, we said yes to Jesus and received Christ as our Savior. Now grace is our king and leads us to eternal life through Jesus Christ our Lord! Glory to God! Thank You, Lord, for Your grace. The grace of God is now to reign in our lives.

In the beginning, Adam was created perfect and put in a perfect world created by a perfect God. God told Adam, *"but of the tree of the knowledge of good and evil you shall not eat, for in the day that you eat of it you shall surely die"* (Gen. 2:17).

This was not immediate physical death, although death did enter the world at that moment. This was spiritual death—separation from God. God will not have sin in His presence. The Holy Spirit would have to depart from Adam in the garden. When Adam rebelled in the garden and ate of the tree, the sin nature entered man, and the acts of sin followed. This sin nature would then be passed on to all mankind. That is why Jesus said, "You must be born again" (John 3:3-6). He was talking about a spiritual rebirth.

> *"Therefore, just as through one man sin entered the world, and death through sin, and thus death spread to all men, because all sinned"* (Rom. 5:12).

Both times, the word *sin* in this verse is the noun *hamartia* for the sin nature.

> *"For all have sinned and fall short of the glory of God"* (Rom. 3:23).

We are all born with the sin nature—*hamartia*—and that is why we have all sinned—*hamartano*. We do not commit the acts of sin and then become a sinner. We are born a sinner, and that is why we sin. We are born with the sin nature.

> *"Behold, I was brought forth in iniquity, And in sin my mother conceived me"* (Ps. 51:5).

The devil gets too much credit for our failures. We say, "Oh, the devil made me do it!" No, we simply tried to defeat the sin nature in the wrong way! The sin nature within us is what produces the acts of sin. The Word of God teaches us how to shut down the sin nature. It is by simple faith in the cross of Christ and nothing else! Only the blood shed on the cross defeats sin. Not our own efforts.

"As it is written: "There is none righteous, no, not one" (Rom. 3:10).

For a believer to live a victorious, overcoming Christian life, he must understand this great truth—that there is nothing good in us. But you might say, "I do a lot of wonderful things in the community." None righteous! "But I go to church and pray for people." None righteous!

Please, allow the Lord to reveal and confirm this great truth to you about the sin nature.

"There is none righteous, no, not one." This includes us Christians. Yes, we now have the righteousness of Christ imputed or given to us. However, within ourselves, there is no good thing! The sooner we identify and acknowledge that the real problem is the sin nature, the sooner we will have victory over it.

How to live for God in plain language:
With grace, not the sin nature, as our king.

HOW TO LIVE FOR GOD
in plain language...

CHAPTER 2

THE STRENGTH OF SIN IS THE LAW

CHAPTER TWO
THE STRENGTH OF SIN IS THE LAW

"The sting of death is sin, and the strength of sin is the law" (I Cor. 15:56).

Learning that the sin nature is man's real problem has given us insight as to why we sin. In this verse, we will now learn how the sin nature is empowered by law—any law.

The Greek word for law, in verse 56 and throughout the Bible, is *nomos*. It is defined as "Anything established by use; a custom or an ordinance," meaning, it can be a law of God or a law of man. Let me state it this way: If we, as Christians, are having a continuous problem with sin, any sin, and we devise a plan to stop sinning, then that plan becomes a law. This law will strengthen the sin nature. The only answer for the sin nature is the shed blood of Jesus on the cross and our faith in that finished work alone.

I cannot tell you how many times I have heard of a person going to their pastor (and this could be you) saying, "Pastor, I love God. I have been born again, serving the Lord for ten years, but I have a problem. I am drinking (gambling, lusting, cursing), and I don't want to do it anymore! I have tried everything, but I can't stop! What do I do, Pastor, what do I do?"

If a pastor does not understand that the cross of Christ was not just for our initial salvation but also where the victory over all sin was won, he will give the poor struggling Christian a "law" that will strengthen the sin nature!

If a pastor says, "Read the Bible, fast, pray, quote Scripture, and you will have victory," no, you will not! That pastor has mistakenly led you into strengthening the sin nature. How is that possible? By turning good Christian disciplines into laws. Reading the Bible is good, for faith comes by hearing and hearing by the word of God. However, that is not how and where sin was defeated. Fasting is biblical. We should fast to seek His face to get direction in our lives, but fasting does not defeat sin. These Christian disciplines now become laws and will only strengthen the sin nature. The only victory over sin is the finished work of the cross! The pastor must point the defeated Christian to Jesus Christ and Him crucified. Why? Because it was on the cross where all sin was taken care of.

If the Christian tries to get victory over sin by a program of man, or faith in anything other than the finished work of the cross, it will only make the sin nature stronger. Things will only get worse for the struggling believer. I would dare to say that we have all experienced this at one time or another. But sadly, we did not know why we were failing.

CHAPTER TWO THE STRENGTH OF SIN IS THE LAW | 19

Today, there are many in the church who are living defeated and miserable lives because they are trying to conquer or gain victory over sin in the wrong way. In plain language, anything we put our faith in other than the finished work of the cross of Christ becomes a law and will strengthen the sin nature.

I would like you to read this book in order, chapter by chapter. When you get to page 146, there is a huge revelation that will be a wonderful blessing to you. But please, do not look ahead to page 146.

There are many programs of man that come and go every few years. Regrettably, they have the opposite effect on the believer than intended. These programs become laws that strengthen the sin nature. These systems devised by man will only lead the believer to a defeated Christian life. These systems that man develops or invents to try to live for God, whether ignorantly or not, become a law for the Christian. The Bible says this will only empower or strengthen the sin nature. Law—any law—is the strength of the sin nature.

> *"For sin* [the sin nature] *shall not have dominion over you, for you are not under law but under grace"* (Rom. 6:14).

This verse in Romans 6 is clear. Please look at it closely and believe it. According to the Bible, if the Christian is struggling with a certain, specific sin over and over, it is because they are trying to defeat sin, the sin nature, by something other than faith in the sacrifice of God's Son. They have gone back to law.

> "But thanks be to God, who gives us the victory through our Lord Jesus Christ" (I Cor. 15:57).

This verse plainly tells us that it is God Himself who gives us the victory over the sin nature through Jesus Christ our Lord. We must keep our faith in His sacrifice on the cross! You might be saying right now, "I have my faith in the cross, but I am still struggling with a sin." Yes, I am sure you have your faith in the cross for salvation, but you are trying to live for God by law.

We have victory over sin by simple faith in the finished work of the cross. There is no other way. There is not a program or system of man that can stop or control the sin nature.

You are reading this right now, and you love God, but you have not received victory over a sin or sins in your life. Believe and receive the Word of God, and you will be made free! Take your faith off the latest book and off your own efforts in trying to defeat this sin problem! Right now, put your faith exclusively in the cross of Christ, His finished work. That is where sin was defeated. The cross of Christ paid for the penalty of sin and also gives the believer the power over sin.

As the old hymn says, "There is power, power, wonder-working power, in the blood of the Lamb!"

> "Therefore, my beloved brethren, be steadfast, immovable, always abounding in the work of the Lord, knowing that your labor is not in vain in the Lord" (I Cor. 15:58).

In this verse, the Holy Spirit is talking to us, the believers, *"Therefore my beloved brethren."* He is telling us to be *"steadfast, immovable, always abounding in the work of the Lord."* What is the work of the Lord? It is His finished work of the cross! We must not look to anything else. If we look to something other than the cross of Jesus, our labor for the Lord will be for nothing. There are many, well-meaning Christians doing wonderful things around the world with much humanitarian effort. Sadly, their labor is in vain because their faith is in their own effort and not in the finished work of Calvary.

> *"For the message of the cross is foolishness to those who are perishing, but to us who are being saved it is the power of God"* (I Cor. 1:18).

What did the Holy Spirit mean when He had the apostle Paul write, *"the message of the cross?"* He was not talking about a wooden beam or a cross-shaped idol around your neck. Of course not. That is not the power of God for the believer. The Holy Spirit is saying that what Jesus did on the cross, by shedding His precious blood, is God's power for us that are saved.

The Christian's power over the devil, the world, the flesh, and the sin nature is the cross of Christ! Hear me, please. The victory Jesus won on the cross is not just for salvation!

The Holy Spirit through Paul is writing to the church in Corinth and to the church today. He is clearly and unquestionably telling us to put our faith back in the sacrifice! This is not popular in many Christian circles because millions are bound or enslaved to a program or system of man. They would have to reject or cast off these programs of man and come back to faith in Christ alone.

The Word of God instructs us to simply believe. All things are possible, only believe. We must ask ourselves the question, was the blood shed by Jesus enough or not? When we believe and receive the message of the cross that the Holy Spirit is teaching throughout the Bible, we will remove most of the books from our libraries, turn off that TV preacher who is selling miracle water or teaching a different way to overcome sin and look only unto Jesus! It is the cross, the cross, the cross! Looking only unto Jesus and His finished work at the cross.

Now let me ask you, did you look ahead to page 146? I gave you one law—don't look ahead to page 146—to show you that even a simple law would strengthen your sin nature. Many of you looked. The few of you who did not look wanted to look, proving that your sin nature was strengthened, activated by a law.

We have learned that the Christian does have a sin nature and that it is strengthened by law—any law.

What I want you to take away from this chapter is the great truth that the law is the strength of the sin nature and the only victory over the sin nature is the shed blood of the Lamb!

How to live for God in plain language:
With our faith exclusively in the cross of Christ!

HOW TO LIVE FOR GOD
in plain language...

CHAPTER 3

LOOKING UNTO JESUS

CHAPTER THREE

LOOKING UNTO JESUS

"Looking unto Jesus, the author and finisher of our faith, who for the joy that was set before Him endured the cross, despising the shame, and has sat down at the right hand of the throne of God" (Hebrews 12:2).

"Looking" in the Greek, *aphorontes*, means to look only to Jesus, but it also means not to look at anything else. We are not to look to a system of man, our denominational rules, ourselves, or the latest fad in the Christian bookstore. We are to be looking exclusively to Jesus Christ and His finished work at the cross. It is at the cross where Jesus paid for everything the Christian needs.

Before we are saved, we are looking to the law, the Ten Commandments, and not Jesus. The law convicts us of our sin. We are then converted, meaning to turn around and go a different way. Now, we are looking to the cross of Christ where sin was paid for.

We cannot look in two directions at the same time. We cannot look to law and to Jesus at the same time. Looking to law strengthens the sin nature. Looking only unto Jesus and His finished work of the cross will bring freedom from the dominion of, and victory over, the sin nature in our lives.

The word *author* in the Greek, *archegos*, is defined as originator, creator. It does not mean to cause us to have faith, but rather, that God is the originator and creator of faith. Notice in this verse that the word *our* is in italics, meaning it was not in the original text but added by the translators for clarity. If we read the verse again and remove the word *our*, it takes on an entirely different meaning: "Looking (exclusively) unto Jesus, the author, (originator, creator) and finisher of faith."

In time and eternity past, the Godhead, through foreknowledge, knew man would sin and would need to be redeemed. God decided that man would be saved by His grace through the faith of the Son of God, Jesus Christ. His faith! For He is the faithful one, the finisher. And where did Jesus finish it? "For the joy set before Him, He endured the cross." He finished faith on the cross! Jesus authored and finished God's plan of salvation through faith at the cross.

We are to live by the same faith that Jesus had. Jesus had faith in His finished work of the cross. That is why He came to earth, to die on the cross. He had faith that it would take away our sin. It was the wisdom of God. He believed it! Jesus was the author of faith, and Jesus was the finisher of faith on the cross. Now our faith must be the faith of the Son of God.

CHAPTER THREE LOOKING UNTO JESUS | 27

> *"And the life which I now live in the flesh I live by the faith of the Son of God, who loved me, and gave himself for me"* (Gal. 2:20, KJV).

In the Old Testament, before the cross, we see it is the faith of the person.

> *"Behold the proud, His soul is not upright in him; But the just shall live by his faith"* (Hab. 2:4).

In the gospels, when Jesus was on the earth, but before He went to the cross, we see, it was still the faith of the person:

> *"Be of good cheer, daughter; your faith has made you well"* (Matt. 9:22).

> *"According to your faith let it be to you"* (Matt. 9:29).

> *"So the Lord said, 'If you have faith as a mustard seed...'"* (Luke 17:6).

> *"Then Jesus said to him, 'Receive your sight; your faith has made you well'"* (Luke 18:42).

Before the cross, the 'one faith' was by promise. But on the cross is where Jesus cried with a loud voice, "It is finished!" Jesus finished faith on the cross! Now, we are to have the same faith that Jesus had, faith in His finished work. Now, the 'one faith' is the finished work of the cross!

> *"There is one body and one Spirit, just as you were called in one hope of your calling; one Lord, one faith, one baptism"* (Eph. 4:4-5).

It is the faith of Jesus. It is His faith, in His finished work of the cross and His faith alone that we must live by. His faith and our faith are to be 'one' in the same or it will be faith that does not please the Father. We must have faith in Jesus' finished work. We must look only unto Jesus.

> *"I am crucified with Christ: nevertheless I live; yet not I, but Christ liveth in me: and the life which I now live in the flesh I live by the faith of the Son of God, who loved me, and gave himself for me"* (Gal. 2:20, KJV).

How to live for God in plain language:
We are to be looking only to the cross of Christ and not to man or programs of man. Faith in anything other than the cross is not faith that God recognizes. It was His faith!

HOW TO LIVE FOR GOD
in plain language...

CHAPTER 4

OUR WILLPOWER IS NOT ENOUGH

CHAPTER FOUR
OUR WILLPOWER IS NOT ENOUGH

"Now if I do what I will not to do, it is no longer I who do it, but sin that dwells in me" (Rom. 7:20).

Once again, we see the Greek word for sin, *hamartia*, a noun, for the sin nature. This verse makes it clear that the sin nature is stronger than our willpower. We are not talking about a once-in-a-while, random act of sin that all believers experience, but rather the sin nature itself that ends up dominating a Christian in some form or another. We tell ourselves, "I'm not going to sin, I'm not going to sin, I'm not going to do that anymore," but then we commit the same sin again. Sound familiar? Nowhere in the Bible does it tell us to fight against sin. We are to fight the good fight of faith! Faith in what? Faith in Jesus' finished work of the cross! It is the cross of Christ that provides both the deliverance from sin and the power over sin. It truly is the double cure, saved from wrath and makes me pure!

Before we look at Paul's testimony in Chapter 7 of Romans, I would like to clear up one thing. The Holy Spirit had the apostle Paul write of his own personal struggle with the sin nature and how he eventually received victory over it. Some say this chapter was the apostle's testimony before salvation. No! Verse 15 says he hated sin. An unsaved man does not hate sin! Paul is relating his struggle with the sin nature as a believer *before* he was given the revelation of the cross for victory over the sin nature.

> *"Or do you not know, brethren (for I speak to those who know the law), that the law has dominion over a man as long as he lives?"* (Rom. 7:1)

The Holy Spirit is saying, "Don't you know that the law will dominate us as long as we live?" We need to know this great truth about dying to the law. The only way to escape the demands of the law will be to die. He is not talking about our physical death but rather a separation that occurs at our conversion. At that moment, we become dead to the law. Our relationship with the law is over!

> *"For Christ is the end of the law for righteousness to everyone who believes"* (Rom. 10:4).

> *"Do not think that I came to destroy the Law or the Prophets. I did not come to destroy but to fulfill"* (Matt. 5:17).

> *"But before faith came, we were kept under guard by the law, kept for the faith which would afterward be revealed. Therefore the law was our tutor to bring us to Christ, that we might be justified by faith. But after faith has come, we are no longer under a tutor"* (Gal. 3:23-25).

The law has done its job by showing us we needed a Savior. Now that we are born-again, we have been released from the law. We are to be dead to the law. Again, this word *dead* does not mean physical death but rather that our relationship with the law has been broken.

> *"For the woman who has a husband is bound by the law to her husband as long as he lives. But if the husband dies, she is released from the law of her husband. So then if, while her husband lives, she marries another man, she will be called an adulteress; but if her husband dies, she is free from that law, so that she is no adulteress, though she has married another man"* (Rom. 7:2-3)

Paul is comparing the bride of Christ to a married woman committing adultery. The Holy Spirit is showing us how destructive it is to our relationship with God when we go back to law. The law is holy and righteous. The law is from God. Before we were saved, we were married to the law and the sin nature was dominating our lives. When we accepted Jesus as our Lord and Savior, we were set free from the law and the sin nature is not to dominate us any longer. We are now married to Christ. We are no longer married to the law!

For example, when I met my wife, she had a boyfriend. Then she met me; we fell in love and were married. She became dead to the boyfriend. The boyfriend is not dead, she is dead to the boyfriend. The relationship is over. The law is not dead but our relationship with the law is over. We are now married to Christ.

Unfortunately, what happens to many Christians is that in a short time, the old boyfriend, the law, comes around, and we commit spiritual adultery by trying to live by law. We must remain dead to the law. Jesus paid for our freedom from the law with His life! How do you think He feels when we go back to law? When we trust in a man-made system, for any need in our life, we are committing spiritual adultery. We are saying that His shed blood on the cross was not enough.

> *"Therefore, my brethren, you also have become dead to the law through the body of Christ, that you may be married to another—to Him who was raised from the dead, that we should bear fruit to God"* (Rom. 7:4).

Paul is saying to born-again believers that the law is no longer for us. We are now dead to the law! Christ's death on the cross broke our relationship with the law. Thank You, Jesus! The law is still there for the unbeliever to bring them to Christ, but for believers, the law is to have no part in our lives.

> *"But we know that the law is good if one uses it lawfully, knowing this: that the law is not made for a righteous person...."* (I Tim. 1:8-9)

We are righteous through faith in the blood that Jesus shed on the cross. We must not commit spiritual adultery by going back to law. Once again, law is anything that we put our trust in other than the cross of Jesus. It can be a law of God, the Ten Commandments, or a law of man. That man can even be ourselves. Yes, we make laws for ourselves in trying to gain victory over sin or in trying to please Him. We must repent of these self-efforts and come back to our first love!

> *"For what I am doing, I do not understand. For what I will to do, that I do not practice; but what I hate, that I do"* (Rom. 7:15).

This is the testimony of every Christian who tries to gain victory over the sin nature by law. Here, Paul is relating his struggle of living the Christian life by trying to keep the law. His sin nature became strengthened, and he did not do the things that he wanted to do, and the things he hated, he did. It is the same for all believers that try to get victory over the sin nature by law. Like Paul, we will end up doing things that we hate! A true, born-again believer does not want to sin! He does not want to fail God!

I will share with you my own personal testimony. I mentioned briefly in the preface of this book my struggle with alcohol a couple of months after I was born-again. There are some Christian circles that would say, "Well, he wasn't really saved." If the qualification for being saved by the blood of Jesus is that we never sin again, then we are all in trouble. We are not righteous and holy before a holy God because we never sin. We are righteous and holy before God the Father because our faith is in Jesus who never sinned!

The problem was, I continued to associate with my old friends in an effort to convert them to this wonderful life I had discovered in Christ. I would stop at the tavern after work as I had in the past but would drink only Pepsi. Before long, I ended up drinking a glass of wine, then two, three, or more glasses of wine. I did not want to drink alcohol; I had been delivered from that evil thing. Bottom line, I ended up trying to defeat this sin the same way the apostle Paul testified about in Romans Chapter 7, by my own willpower.

I hated this sin! I would go to church on Sunday, then turn around and get drunk during the week. I had no power in my own strength to say no! Unfortunately, I had not been taught to deny self and look only to Jesus and His shed blood for victory over sin. I brought reproach upon the name of the Lord and ruined my testimony.

Finally, after one more night of drinking, I got up and cried out to God, "I can't do this!" I heard the Holy Spirit, in that still, small voice say, "Good, it's about time! You cannot defeat sin, Jesus defeated sin for you. Put your faith in the cross of Christ!" The Holy Spirit was telling me to stop fighting sin and start fighting the fight of faith!

As Jeremiah said, *"Ask for the old paths, where the good way is, and walk in it; then you will find rest for your souls"* (Jer. 6:16).

Well, let me tell you, my joy returned, my peace returned, and I was once again resting in the cross of Jesus. I had victory from that day until now! I have not had a drink of alcohol since—not even a fleeting desire!

DELIVERANCE THROUGH FAITH IN THE BLOOD!

My pastor told me to just stop drinking. He did not know that the cross had paid for all sin—past, present, and, God forbid, even future sin. But with faith placed only in the finished work of the cross, I am now pure and holy in His sight.

This is why the Christian bookstores are overflowing with hundreds of books telling us how to live free from sin. There are not hundreds or even dozens of ways to live for God. There is only one way, and it is by faith in Jesus Christ and Him crucified! Thank You, Jesus, for giving Your life to defeat this sin in my life.

I was trying with my own willpower to defeat sin. I had become a spiritual adulterer. The apostle Paul learned that his willpower was not strong enough to stop him from sinning. He had become a spiritual adulterer. He had put his faith back in law to try to live for God.

In the next chapter, we will look at the victory side of Paul's Romans 7 testimony. We must believe the great truth that we cannot live for God by our own willpower. We cannot defeat sin in our own strength.

How to live for God in plain language:
We live for God by faith in the cross alone, the sacrifice of God's Son or we become spiritual adulterers.

HOW TO LIVE FOR GOD
in plain language...

CHAPTER 5

THE WRETCHED MAN MOMENT

CHAPTER FIVE
THE WRETCHED MAN MOMENT

Looking further into the testimony of the great man of God, the apostle Paul, we will learn how he received victory over the things he did not want to do.

> *"For what I am doing, I do not understand. For what I will to do, that I do not practice; but what I hate, that I do"* (Rom. 7:15).

The struggling Christian's only source of victory over the sin nature is the cross of Christ. Jesus won the victory for us over the devil, the flesh, and the sin nature. We that are born again, like Paul, hate sin. As he stated in verse 15, his willpower was not enough to stop him from doing the things he hated. If you are struggling with a recurring sin and hate the thing you are doing (like the apostle Paul) and do not understand what is wrong, then let the Word of God show you today how to live for God! You will need to stop looking to your own efforts, or another Christian program. You are to look only to the cross of Christ where sin was defeated.

> *"If then, I do what I will not to do, I agree with the law that it is good. But now, it is no longer I who do it, but sin that dwells in me"* (Rom. 7:16-17).

The law is from God. The law is holy. The law is not the problem. The law is good, and we should love the law of God. But as we will see, the law gives us no power over the sin nature. The law had a very specific purpose. The law did its job in our lives when it brought us to Jesus. If we look again to a law, any law, to defeat sin, we will only worsen the situation. We need to let the Holy Spirit reveal this to us, as He did to Paul. When we are struggling and practicing the things we do not want to do, it is because the sin nature has been revived, due to the law being the strength of the sin nature (I Cor. 15:56).

We are not talking about an occasional sin, but a particular sin or sins that occur over and over in the life of a Christian. When this happens, whether we know it or not, we have gone back to law to try to defeat sin. The sin nature is now dominating that area of our lives. You might say, "I'm not sure about this. I have never heard this." Please continue to read and believe the testimony of the apostle Paul in the Word of God.

CHAPTER FIVE THE WRETCHED MAN MOMENT

> *"For I know that in me, (that is in my flesh), nothing good dwells; for to will is present with me, but how to perform what is good I do not find"* (Rom. 7:18).

This verse is all important for us in furthering our understanding of how to live a holy life. There is nothing good in us! The desire to do what is right is not enough.

We need to hear and believe that. Read verse 18 again. My wife Dorene occasionally shares her testimony about not being "good." She was always a good girl, top of her class, went to church regularly, did not get into trouble, etc. Then, at twenty-eight years old, she was convicted of her sin and gave her life to Jesus. She was born again! When she read the verse that says there is none good (Rom. 3:12), she had a conversation with God that went something like this: "God, I know Your Word is true, and it says there is nothing good in me, but it feels like there is still good in me. Please show me what you mean." When the Holy Spirit began to open up the message of the cross to her, she saw herself in the light of the cross, and everything changed. She now knew that there was nothing good in her, and she began to grow in the grace and knowledge of Him. This is what happened to the apostle Paul and what needs to happen to every believer in order to learn how to live for God.

From the fall in the garden, when the sin nature entered man, we have had nothing good in us. Once again, we must understand this all-important truth, that there is nothing good in us, in order to get to the place where we are completely dependent on the sacrifice of God's Son. Let us go back to Paul's testimony.

> *"For the good that I will to do, I do not do; but the evil I will not to do, that I practice. Now if I do what I will not to do, it is no longer I who do it, but the sin that dwells in me"* (Rom. 7:19-20).

The word *practice* in the Greek means "dominion." The sin nature is now dominating this great man of God. It cannot be any clearer than that. The apostle Paul is saying that the sin nature in me is overriding my willpower. The devil is not mentioned in the first eight chapters of Romans. The devil cannot override our free will. If he could, he would have us all kill ourselves. No, it is not Satan that "made me do it," It is the sin nature that we inherited from Adam that is the Christian's greatest enemy.

Like Paul, when we are struggling with a particular sin that we are practicing and hate, we too must recognize and admit that our willpower is not enough to stop the sin. We also need to embrace the truth that a law of any kind will strengthen that sin. I can hear some right now saying, "I have Christ in me, and I can stop this sin." Then why haven't you? Because you are looking to yourself and some foolish man-made law to defeat what Jesus has already defeated on the cross! We are talking about having a revelation of the message of the cross that is the power of God for the Christian (I Cor. 1:18). The only victory over sin is the cross! We must take our faith off of ourselves, off of that new Christian program and come back to faith in Jesus Christ and Him crucified. Then and only then will we experience the abundant, overcoming life Jesus promised.

> *"I find then a law, that evil is present with me, the one who wills to do good. For I delight in the law of God according to the inward man"* (Rom. 7:21-22).

As Christians, we should always agree with the Bible. When the Word of God says that we have evil present with us, we must believe it. Again, this is an all-important truth that we Christians must accept in order for us to learn how to live for God.

> *"But I see another law in my members, warring against the law of my mind, and bringing me into captivity to the law of sin which is in my members"* (Rom. 7:23).

There is a war going on between our minds and our members where the sin nature dwells. Read the verse closely. My mind says, "Don't look at that pornography; it is a sin before the Lord." But my members—my eyes where the sin nature dwells—want to look. My mind says, "Don't go into that place anymore; you're a Christian now." But my members—my feet where the sin nature dwells—take me in there. The sin nature in my members is warring against my mind and is winning the battle because I am trying to stop sinning by my own willpower or some foolish program of man. The popular forty-day plan or encounter groups are powerless against the law of sin! Psychology tries to talk us out of sinning and the Christian community comes up with hundreds of carnal ways in an attempt to defeat the sin nature. However, they do not understand that these are spiritual laws that will never be defeated by our flesh. What is the answer? Read on, the answer is in the Word.

> *"O wretched man that I am! Who will deliver me from this body of death?" (Rom. 7:24).*

Finally, the apostle Paul cries out for help from above, "Who will deliver me?" Not *what* will deliver me! Our deliverance from the things that we hate and do not want to do does not come from a foolish program. Our deliverance and victory comes from a *who*. But only when we know that we are wretched, and not until.

This word *wretched*, in the Greek, has the root meaning of "exhausted from labor." When we get to the end of ourselves and in our heart of hearts recognize that we cannot live for God in our own strength and ability and cry out to a holy God, then and only then will the answer come!

This is the message of the cross revealed! Paul cries out for a who! If you go to the Christian bookstore, you will find a thousand different books with a thousand different ways to have victory in your life. But we have the one book, the Bible, and the one way, Jesus! He said, "I am the way!" Jesus is the who!

> *"I thank God—through Jesus Christ our Lord! So then, with the mind I myself serve the law of God, but with the flesh the law of sin" (Rom. 7:25).*

The answer is Jesus Christ! And how did He deliver us from sin? By going to the cross. It is finished! Glory to God!

Paul now knows why he is failing. He has had the wretched man moment, realizing that he is exhausted from trying to live for God in his own strength, and he cries out to God, "Who shall deliver me?" With his mind, he was serving the law of God, but in his flesh, the law of sin. How do you and I live for God? We simply cry out, "I can't do this, but I thank God that through Jesus Christ and His finished work of the cross, I have power over sin in my life!"

> *"For the message of the cross is foolishness to those who are perishing, but to us who are being saved it is the power of God" (I Cor. 1:18).*

The crucifixion of Jesus is foolishness to the unredeemed man. An unbeliever thinks, "What does a man who died two thousand years ago have to do with me?" But to us who are saved, it is the power of God! Power over the flesh, power over the devil, power over the world, and power over the sin nature. We do not fight the sin nature, the devil, or the flesh. We fight the good fight of faith! That faith must not be in a man or in ourselves. Our faith must remain in the shed blood of Jesus. Glory to God!

So, let me recap this all-important testimony of the apostle Paul in Romans 7. He says we are married to Christ, and if we go back to our old husband—the law—we become spiritual adulterers.

What is law? Anything that is not faith in Jesus Christ and Him crucified. The Bible tells us that law, any law, will strengthen the sin nature. When we trust in anything else for victory, we have gone back to law, and we will not do the things that we will. We will do the things we hate. "Well, I don't believe that!" Then you have not had your wretched man moment when you realized that you are struggling with the sin nature and not living the abundant life Jesus promised. You need to cry out to Jesus Christ instead of going to a law for victory. The cross is not just for salvation. We need to know that we are wretched!

There are only two times the word *wretched* is used in the Bible. The first, as we have just studied, is when the apostle Paul came to the end of himself and knew he was exhausted from trying to live for God in his own strength, by law. The only other time the Holy Spirit used the word *wretched* was when Jesus was speaking to the church of the Laodiceans.

CHAPTER FIVE THE WRETCHED MAN MOMENT | 49

"Because you say, 'I am rich, have become wealthy, and have need of nothing'—and do not know that you are wretched, miserable, poor, blind and naked" (Rev. 3:17).

The born-again believers of today's Christian church are like the church of the Laodiceans. They do not realize they are trying to sanctify themselves by the programs of man. They do not know that they are wretched!

Until you have that wretched man moment, you will be exhausted from trying to defeat the sin nature by law rather than by faith in the finished work of Jesus on the cross. The moment you move your faith back to the finished work of Jesus, you will begin to live the abundant life that Jesus promised. Glory to God!

How to live for God in plain language:
Know that you are wretched and cry out to the Who to deliver you!

HOW TO LIVE FOR GOD
in plain language...

CHAPTER 6

DENY SELF AND DIE

CHAPTER SIX

DENY SELF AND DIE

"*Then He said to them all, 'If anyone desires to come after Me, let him deny himself, and take up his cross daily, and follow Me'*" (Luke 9:23).

I am sure that your desire is to follow Jesus, but how? Here is Jesus talking to the multitude, and He says, *"Let him deny himself."* What did Jesus mean? Did He mean to deny yourself nice clothing or food to eat? No. Sadly, there are entire denominations that teach self-denial is holiness. For example, the Amish ride in horse-drawn buggies and have no running water or electricity in their homes. They believe they are more holy and pleasing to God by denying themselves these conveniences. Nothing could be further from the truth. God has blessed us with these things. He is a loving and faithful Father.

Jesus is stating that if we want to come after Him, then we must deny self! We must deny our own efforts, our own wisdom, and our own way. We cannot live for Him in our own strength. Our willpower is not strong enough to live a holy life before a holy God.

Jesus declares, *"If anyone desires to come after Me,"* he must *"take up his cross daily."* It is the believer's cross to die on. In Roman times, when a man was sentenced to death, he would be crucified. He would say goodbye to his family and friends and many times be taken away without his clothes. He would no longer need his clothes; he was going to die! Jesus is saying, if you want to come after Him, you cannot do it in your own strength or willpower. We must deny our own wisdom and man's ways. We are now crucified with Christ and must understand it is no longer we who live. Our life is not our own; we were bought with a price. The precious blood of Jesus has delivered us from sin, from law, from the world and from self! Jesus continues to say in verse 24, *"For whoever desires to save his life will lose it, but whoever loses his life for My sake will save it"* (Luke 9:24).

We cannot save ourselves. We cannot follow Jesus by carnal means. We must die! Go ahead and die to your self-efforts and law. It is a good death! The Christian must lose his life and die to self to live a victorious, overcoming, Christian life.

Yet man does not want to hear this. We do not want to die to our ideas of how to live for God. What could be wrong with a forty-day, purpose-driven system devised by man? The writer is just trying to help man, right? However well-intentioned these programs of man are, they point us to ourselves as the power source. In 99 percent of these programs of man, we are not taught to deny self as Jesus instructed. But rather, to look to self! "You do this on Day 8; you do this on Day 22, etc." Me, me, me! These systems of man are not Christ-centered but self-centered.

I was teaching a class a few years ago at a Bible college in the Philippines. I asked the question, "After I complete my forty-day program, what am I supposed to do on Day 41?" An eighteen-year-old, first-year student on the front row answered, "Rest day!" Rest from the forty days of law! She better understood what Jesus said regarding denying self than most theologians. On the cross Jesus said, "It is finished!" The work is done. We must deny self and rest in His finished work.

Is Jesus saying that we do not do *anything*? Of course not! Stop with that foolish thinking! We do many Christian disciplines. But we must not put our faith in what we do. Jesus is saying we cannot do anything to make ourselves holy. It is totally and completely by faith in what He accomplished on the cross! Jesus is teaching us to die every day, then follow Him!

Over and over, the Scriptures tell us not to look to the flesh. Man will let us down every time. But praise God, the blood of Jesus will never fail! Our faith must remain in Jesus Christ and Him crucified. Not just Jesus, but His sacrifice on the cross. That is where the victory was won! Victory over the devil, the flesh, the law, the sin, and the world! "The just shall live by his faith!" Faith in what? A twelve-step program?

Twenty-one days of fasting? No! Faith exclusively in what Christ did for us on the cross, the finished work of Jesus.

Once again, we must understand that these programs and systems of man end up becoming laws to us. We are to live under grace alone. Not grace and law. We must not, cannot, mix law with God's grace!

> *"I have been crucified with Christ; it is no longer I who live, but Christ lives in me; and the life which I now live in the flesh I live by faith of the Son of God, who loved me and gave Himself for me"* (Gal. 2:20).

This is not simply good doctrine; it is the apostle Paul's testimony.

Why did the Holy Spirit have Paul write *"crucified with Christ"*? In the mind of God, every believer who has been born again by faith in the shed blood of Jesus, was in Christ on the cross. We died with Christ. What an amazing truth! God sees us as, *"crucified with Christ; it is no longer I who live"*!

We will never live a victorious Christian life until we understand what the apostle Paul is testifying here. He said, *"It is no longer I who live."* He denied self! He will no longer look to himself for anything!

But wait a minute! Some say, "We must do something!" Yes! We must always keep our faith in the sacrifice of God's Son. "But, what about works? Are there works for the Christian to do?" Absolutely!

> *"But someone will say, 'You have faith, and I have works.' Show me your faith without your works, and I will show you my faith by my works"* (James 2:18).

"I will show you my faith by my works." The Holy Spirit is clearly giving the example of Abraham offering up his son, his only son, Isaac, the same as God the Father did by offering up Jesus, His only Son. Because his faith was in God, he was able to take Isaac up on that mountain to sacrifice him. Abraham's faith produced the works! Proper faith will always produce proper works. It is not the other way around. Works will not produce faith. Faith must always come first! Faith, correctly placed, will be in Jesus Christ and His finished work of the cross, not in the latest book in the Christian bookstore.

This truth of the patriarch Abraham going to offer his son Isaac is one of the greatest examples of self-denial in the Bible. Abraham had to die to his own understanding and be obedient to the faith. God told Abraham to take his son Isaac and sacrifice him. He was not instructed to take Ishmael, who was a result of the flesh. But to take Isaac, the promised son from God, a type of Jesus, the only begotten Son of God. Jesus is totally of God! Abraham (the Father), took Isaac (the son), up on the mountain, a type of Mount Calvary. Isaac, the son, carried the wood, a type of Jesus carrying the cross. Isaac then asks his father, "Where is the sacrifice?" Abraham answered and said, "God will provide Himself a Lamb." That is faith! Next comes the works.

Abraham laid his son, a type of Jesus, on the wood, a type of the cross, and raised the knife to take the life of his son. But God said, "Abraham, Abraham, do not harm the boy." At that moment, Abraham saw a ram caught in the thicket by its horns. This ram was the substitution. Jesus, instead of you and me. Glory to God! Because Abraham had faith in God, he showed us his works. Every step Abraham took towards that mountain where he would sacrifice his son was his works. Works follow faith.

Thank You, Father, that your Son was obedient unto death, even the death of the cross (Phil 2:8). Help me not to look to myself. Show me, Father, how to die to all my abilities and to lose my life for Your sake that I may live the abundant life You promised. Glory to Your name!

How to live for God in plain language:
Deny self-effort and die—every day!
No death, no resurrected life!

HOW TO LIVE FOR GOD
in plain language...

CHAPTER 7

OBEDIENCE

CHAPTER SEVEN
OBEDIENCE

What is our obedience? What a question! We have many answers, but we must go to the Word of God for the true answer.

> *"For as by one man's disobedience many were made sinners..."* (Rom. 5:19).

Do not let the English word *many*, confuse you. It means all, everyone. The one man whose disobedience made everyone a sinner was Adam.

> *"But of the tree of the knowledge of good and evil you shall not eat, for in the day that you eat of it you shall surely die"* (Gen. 2:17).

Adam disobeyed and ate of the tree. At that moment, the sin nature entered the world, and now the sin nature has been passed down to all men.

> *"Therefore, just as through one man sin entered the world, and death through sin, and thus death spread to all men, because all sinned"* (Rom. 5:12).

Once again, the word *sin* in this verse is the noun, the sin nature. We are all born with the sin nature. We do not sin and become a sinner; we are born with the sin nature, and that is why we sin.

> *"So also by one Man's obedience many will be made righteous"* (Rom. 5:19).

Righteous means that we always did what was right in the eyes of God. The one Man here is, of course, Jesus Christ. Jesus is the only perfect and righteous one. Jesus kept the law and never sinned. Yet Him keeping the law and never sinning were not the obedience that made us righteous, in and of themselves. So how did Jesus make us righteous?

> *"And being found in appearance as a man, He humbled Himself and became obedient to the point of death, even the death of the cross"* (Phil. 2:8).

What was the will of the Father for His Son? To go to the cross! What was the obedience of Christ that made us righteous? His dying on the cross! Jesus humbled Himself and was obedient to give His life on the cross to make us righteous. No man took His life, He gave it freely (John 10:18). He could have come down from the cross, but He stayed there and let them crucify Him in obedience to the Father's will. It is that obedience—Him laying down His life on the cross and that alone—which makes us righteous! Adam's disobedience made us all sinners; Christ's obedience—the cross—made us righteous. Thank You, Jesus!

> *"Through Him we have received grace and apostleship for obedience to the faith among all nations for His name"* (Rom. 1:5).

What is our obedience now that we are saved? Our obedience to the faith makes us righteous and holy before God. It is not going to church, although we should not forsake the assembling together (Heb. 10:25); or through Bible reading, although faith comes by hearing and hearing by the Word of God (Rom. 10:17). These good Christian disciplines do not make us righteous! It is our obedience to the faith!

Without faith it is impossible to please God (Heb. 11:6). But that faith must have the correct object, the cross! The only faith that God will recognize is faith in the finished work of His Son. It is through Jesus. Everything comes through

Jesus! We receive grace through the sacrifice of Jesus so we might be obedient to the faith!

At this point you might ask, "Is this entire book going to point to the cross of Christ for everything?" Yes, this book will follow the example of the Bible. The cross, the blood, the sacrifice, and the altar. The Bible, from Genesis to Revelation, is all about Jesus Christ *and* Him crucified. The Bible and God Himself points us only to the sacrifice of His Son. God only preaches one message—the message of the cross. All doctrine is founded on the cross of Christ.

How to live for God in plain language:
By being obedient to the faith. The only obedience that makes us holy and acceptable to God is faith in the sacrifice of His Son. That obedience brings glory to God in all nations.

HOW TO LIVE FOR GOD

in plain language...

CHAPTER 8

SEPARATED TO THE GOSPEL

CHAPTER EIGHT

SEPARATED TO THE GOSPEL

"*Paul, a bondservant of Jesus Christ, called to be an apostle, separated to the gospel of God*" (Rom. 1:1).

This word *bondservant*, in the Greek, means "a slave by choice." We used to be a slave of the devil. We used to be a slave of the sin nature. Now we choose to be a slave of Jesus. In Roman times, a slave would be purchased for a period of time, maybe twenty years. After his obligation of twenty years was fulfilled, he was free to leave. However, he had the choice of remaining with his master. A slave by choice! As a believer, we are slaves, servants of Christ, by choice! Paul is making the point that we are called to be a slave first, then called to be an apostle, or pastor, or worship leader, etc.

He continues by saying that we are to be separated to the gospel. This word *separated* means to be separated "to" something. It also means to be separated "from" something. The definition in the Greek means we are to set boundaries around and protect the gospel. We are to keep other things from coming into our lives that are not the gospel. Nothing else must be allowed to come in and compete with the gospel. In other words, the Christian world today gives us many choices to put our faith in, but there is only one true gospel! Only one way!

> *"Jesus said to him, "I am the way, the truth, and the life. No one comes to the Father except through Me"* (John 14:6).

We must be very careful to be separated only to the sacrifice of God's Son. We must not let other things move our faith. The one true gospel is Jesus Christ and Him crucified. Yes, He was born of a virgin and performed miracles, and He still does today, but that was not the "good news" that saved us. He walked the perfect sinless life. He had to be sinless in order to be the spotless sacrifice God demanded to pay for our sin, but that is not what took away our sin. We are to be separated to His finished work of the cross; that is the heart of the gospel and what we are to set boundaries around and protect. We know He rose from the dead on the third day, but it was on the cross where He said, "It is finished!"

The gospel has never changed. What was the gospel, the good news, for Adam? God told him the day that he ate of the Tree of the Knowledge of Good and Evil, he would surely die. He did not drop dead physically, but he did die spiritually. The Holy Spirit had to leave him. God will not have sin in His presence, so Adam had a big problem! He knew he was naked—naked to the judgement of God. What did Adam do? He sewed fig leaves to try to cover and hide his nakedness from God (Gen. 3:7). The fig leaves are a type of religion, man trying to hide his sin from God. Man continues to come up with many forms of fig leaves today, trying to clean himself up and hide his sin from a holy God. With Adam, we see the grace and mercy of God in action. Mercy is simply man not receiving what he deserves. Adam deserved death; we deserve death.

> *"For the wages of sin is death* [the mercy of God did not take Adam's physical life] *but the gift of God is eternal life in Christ Jesus our Lord"* (Rom. 6:23).

Eternal life is a gift. By grace we have been saved! The simple definition of grace is receiving what we do not deserve. We do not deserve that God would send His only begotten Son to pay the sin debt we could not pay. So again, what was the gospel? What is the good news for Adam?

> *"Also for Adam and his wife the Lord God made tunics of skin, and clothed them"* (Gen. 3:21).

For God to provide the skin, He had to shed the blood and take the life of an innocent animal. So right there, in the garden of Eden, God instituted the sacrifice. The sacrifice pointed to what Jesus would do on the cross.

> "...*without the shedding of blood there is no remission* [of sin] (Heb. 9:22).

Thank You, Father, for Your mercy and grace by not taking my life but instead providing the sacrifice of Your Son for my sin.

We are speaking about the gospel, the good news, that we are to be separated to. The gospel has never changed. In the story of Cain and Abel, Cain offered up the fruit of his own labor. He went to the correct altar, but he brought the wrong sacrifice. Sound familiar today? Cain's offering was rejected. You need to hear that one more time! Yes, Cain went to the altar to sacrifice, yet he was not obedient to bring the sacrifice that God would accept!

What is your sacrifice, my brother or sister? God told Cain that his brother Abel had offered up the more excellent sacrifice, the shed blood of the lamb. Abel's sacrifice pointed to Jesus, the Lamb of God, who would take away the sin of the world through His shed blood on the cross! The gospel for Abel was the same as it is for us. The innocent would have to die for the guilty. We must be careful to bring only the blood of Jesus to the altar and nothing else! The gospel from Genesis to the book of Revelation is the same. We are to be separated to the one and only true gospel.

> "*Afterward Moses and Aaron went in and told Pharaoh, 'Thus says the Lord God of Israel: Let My people go,*

that they may hold a feast to Me in the wilderness'" (Ex. 5:1).

The children of Israel were slaves in Egypt for 400 years! Just like them, we were bound by sin and slaves of the devil until we received Christ. God told Moses, "Go tell Pharaoh, Let My people go!"

Pharaoh is a type of the devil. Miracle after miracle, Pharaoh would not let God's people go. Miracles do not save us from our sin. The Bible tells us when Pharaoh finally did let God's people go. It was when God told Moses, "Tell My people to sacrifice an innocent lamb and put the blood on the door post and header of their house and when I see the blood, I will pass over you" (Ex. 12:13).

This is a perfect and clear type and shadow of the cross of our Lord and Savior Jesus Christ. The Word of God tells us that the death angel came that night and the firstborn in all of Egypt died, but the children of God, after 400 years of slavery, were set free!

Chapter twelve of Exodus shows us that the gospel has never changed. We are to be separated to the one and only gospel. Nothing else can deliver us, heal us, or break the bondage of sin. There is one gospel, the only gospel, Jesus Christ and Him crucified! We must be obedient to the faith, separate ourselves, and keep our faith exclusively in the finished work of Christ! Christians must be careful to never move the focus of their faith. The apostle Paul said, *"But God forbid that I should boast except in the cross of our Lord Jesus Christ, by whom the world has been crucified to me, and I to the world*" (Gal. 6:14).

Thank You, Jesus, for Your obedience unto death, even the death of the cross!

How to live for God in plain language:
By remaining separated to the gospel of God.

HOW TO LIVE FOR GOD

in plain language...

CHAPTER 9

BAPTIZED INTO CHRIST

CHAPTER NINE

BAPTIZED INTO CHRIST

The word *baptism* in the Greek simply means "to be immersed." We can be baptized in many ways according to the Word of God. For example, baptized (immersed) into water; baptized (immersed) into the Holy Spirit; or baptized (immersed) into Christ. In this chapter, our focus is on being baptized into Christ.

The understanding of being baptized into Christ on the cross, has changed the lives of millions as the Holy Spirit has opened up this great truth to them. My prayer is that God will use this teaching to show believers what really happened to all of us at the time of our conversion. We will take our study from Romans 6.

As we read Romans 6, every time we see the word *sin*, we should read it as the sin nature. It is used as a noun sixteen times in this chapter, and only in Romans 6:15 is it used as a verb referring to the acts of sin.

> *"What shall we say then? Shall we continue in sin that grace may abound? Certainly not! How shall we who died to sin live any longer in it?"* (Rom. 6:1-2).

In verses one and two, the apostle Paul asks an obviously leading question. Should we continue with the sin nature ruling and reigning so that more grace may abound in our lives? Certainly not! The Holy Spirit is saying, "Do not even think like that!" A true believer does not want to let the sin nature reign in their lives.

Look at the rest of the second verse. We are to be dead to the sin nature because we are in Christ. The sin nature did not die, it is still within us. We have died to the sin nature. However, it is not to reign in our lives. Just as we learned that our relationship with the law was broken because we are dead to the law, our relationship with the sin nature is broken because we are dead to the sin nature. The grace of God has broken our relationship with the sin nature.

> *"Or do you not know that as many of us as were baptized into Christ Jesus were baptized into His death?"* (Rom. 6:3).

The Holy Spirit is saying, we need to know that we were baptized, immersed into Christ's death on the cross. It is an amazing revelation when we know and believe that in the mind of God, we were in Christ on the cross.

CHAPTER NINE BAPTIZED INTO CHRIST | 77

This understanding will take the pressure off the believer to perform for God. When we die to self-effort, die to the law, and die to the sin nature, we are set free! A dead man does not have a problem with sin. If you pass alcohol in front of a dead man, he will have no reaction. A dead man does not fight against the sin nature.

We were baptized, immersed, into the death of Jesus on the cross. The old man died with Christ. We were crucified with Christ. It is no longer us that live. Our relationship with the sin nature is now broken. When the believer is tempted by an old sin such as lusting, drugs, immorality, or alcohol, he must not fight against that evil desire. Instead, because we are dead to the sin nature and alive with Christ, we fight the good fight of faith. Faith in the finished work of Christ on the cross where sin was defeated.

Knowing that the sin nature was defeated over two thousand years ago on the cross will keep you from running to a man-made system when a sin temptation arises in your life. The cross is the answer for all sin! Our faith in Christ's finished work gives us the victory over sin.

It is a law. We will learn more about this great truth in the chapter entitled, "The Law of the Spirit" (Rom. 8:2).

> "Therefore we were buried with Him through baptism into death, that just as Christ was raised from the dead by the glory of the Father, even so we also should walk in newness of life. For if we have been united together in the likeness

of His death, certainly we also shall be in the likeness of His resurrection" (Rom. 6:4-5).

The cross! We died with Christ, we were buried with Christ, and we were raised with Christ. At this point in Romans 6, we should be getting the picture. Our growing in the grace and knowledge of Him cannot be truly measured until we die to self, die to law, and die to the sin nature. As we learned in an earlier chapter, Jesus said we must deny self, take up the cross daily, and die to our own efforts (Luke 9:23).

In Romans 6:5, the word *if* may be exchanged for the word *since*. Since we have been united together with Him at His death on the cross, we were then resurrected together with Christ. Without a death, there can be no resurrection or newness of life. Our resurrected, abundant life is in Christ!

> *"Even when we were dead in trespasses, made us alive together with Christ (by grace you have been saved), and raised us up together, and made us sit together in the heavenly places in Christ Jesus"* (Eph. 2:5-6).

We were *together* with Him on the cross. Made alive together with Christ, raised up together with Him and now we are seated in heavenly places together with Christ Jesus. Wow! In the mind of God, we are already seated in Christ, in heaven, by grace through faith. When the Father looks down on us, He sees us as crucified with His Son, raised with Jesus, and now seated at His right hand together with Christ. Glory to God and the Lamb forever!

How do we live for God in plain language? By knowing that we died with Christ on the cross. Are you dead yet— dead to sin, dead to law, crucified with Christ?

> *"Knowing this, that our old man was crucified with Him, that the body of sin might be done away with, that we should no longer be slaves of sin"* (Rom. 6:6).

The Holy Spirit is telling us that we need to know this! In the mind of God, we were in Jesus when He was on the cross. We died with Him. The old man has been crucified with Him, and we are no longer slaves of the sin nature. That is how and where the sin nature was defeated—on the cross. This is how the sanctification process is allowed to work in our lives. Not by the Christian doing a program or any man-made system and not by fighting against the sin nature. These things put us back in bondage. The cross of Christ has made us free, and we are no longer slaves of the sin nature to obey it in its lusts. Glory to God! Every believer needs to know that the "old man was crucified with Christ."

> *"For he who has died has been freed from sin. Now if we died with Christ, we believe that we shall also live with Him"* (Rom. 6:7-8).

Remember, the word *if* has the meaning of "since." Since we died with Christ on the cross, were buried with Christ, resurrected with Christ, we shall now also live with Him. He defeated death, hell, and the grave. As long as our faith remains in His atoning, redeeming, finished work of the cross, we have the same victory. Praise God! This is really good news for the Christian because now we can conduct our lives accordingly.

We now know how to have victory over the sin nature! By dying to the sin nature and keeping our faith in the finished work of Jesus and nothing else. So now, when we as Christians are faced with an evil desire, we will recognize what is happening and know how to have victory over that evil desire. We will not attempt to defeat that thing in our own willpower, or by a system of man, but will know that Jesus defeated the sin nature on the cross, and we were in Him, and His victory is our victory!

Are you dead to the sin nature yet? Stay dead! A dead man has no problem with sin. When we are saved, we are set free from the penalty of sin. Then, when we understand the cross for our progressive sanctification, taught here in Romans 6, we are set free from the power of sin. Since we died with Christ, we can now live the abundant, resurrected life Jesus promised. But if no death, then no resurrection! Sound simple? Yes, but not that easy to do.

> *"Knowing that Christ, having been raised from the dead, dies no more. Death no longer has dominion over Him.*

For the death that He died, he died to sin once for all; but the life that He lives, He lives to God" (Rom. 6:9-10).

We have victory over death in Christ. He did it for us. He never broke the law. Because we are in Him, God considers us to be perfect law keepers. Jesus did not become a sinner on the cross. He became our sin bearer. He took our sin upon Him, and He defeated sin on the cross by giving His perfect, sinless life for ours. Scholars call this the doctrine of substitution. His life for ours. Glory to God and the Lamb forever!

> *"For what the law could not do in that it was weak through the flesh, God did by sending His own Son in the likeness of sinful flesh, on account of sin: He condemned sin in the flesh"* (Rom. 8:3).

He came in the likeness of sinful flesh, not as a sinner, but as the substitution for our sinful flesh. He condemned sin in the flesh. He did not condemn the believer. He condemned sin! Thank You, Jesus! *"There is therefore now no condemnation to those who are in Christ Jesus"* (Rom. 8:1). Glory to God and the Lamb forever! We deserved death. *"The wages of sin is death, but the gift of God is eternal life in Christ Jesus our Lord"* (Rom. 6:23). Do you see it? We were in Christ on the cross, baptized into His death, raised to newness of life in Christ!

> *"Likewise you also, reckon yourselves to be dead indeed to sin, but alive to God in Christ Jesus our Lord. Therefore do not let sin reign in your mortal body, that you should obey it in its lusts"* (Rom. 6:11-12).

This word *reckon* in verse 11 is an accounting term. It means "to add it up, figure it out, do the math, to conclude." We are to be dead to the sin nature and alive in Christ. By now, hopefully, you have seen clearly that it is all about Jesus Christ and His finished work of the cross. In Christ! Crucified with Christ! In Jesus! Baptized into His death! *"I have been crucified with Christ; it is no longer I who live, but Christ lives in me"* (Gal. 2:20).

In verse 12 it says, do not let the sin nature control you. Before we came to Christ, the sin nature was the king of our flesh, and we obeyed it. Our willpower was not strong enough to fight against the sin nature. We tried to live a clean, holy life, but we could not because the sin nature was our king.

But now, we have been crucified with Christ and our faith is in His finished work of the cross and not in our own willpower. We are dead to what previously dominated us. Now we must remain dead to what dominated our old man, or we will have an unholy revival! Once again, that is why Jesus told us to deny self-effort and take up our cross and die every day (Luke 9:23).

> *"And do not present your members as instruments of unrighteousness to sin, present yourselves to God as being*

alive from the dead, and your members as instruments of righteousness to God" (Rom. 6:13).

The great truth in this verse, if you will understand and believe it, can change your Christian walk. The Holy Spirit is now going to have Paul write how to live for God!

First, we notice that it is not by any law or man's effort whatsoever. We simply do not yield or present our members as instruments of unrighteousness. Our eyes will not look at that which is ungodly, our ears will not listen to ungodly music, and our feet will not take us to places we have no business going to as a Christian. These are not laws. This is the benefit of being crucified with Christ and dead to the sin nature.

The Holy Spirit goes on to tell us that we should present our members as instruments of righteousness to God. We will use our eyes to read the Bible, our ears to hear Christ-centered preaching, and our feet to take us to church. Now we are presenting our members as instruments of righteousness because we are alive from the dead and living the resurrected life in Christ. Glory to God! The abundant life!

"For sin shall not have dominion over you, for you are not under law but under grace" (Rom. 6:14).

The Holy Spirit is making it clear that the sin nature shall not dominate the Christian that was crucified with Christ. Thank You, Jesus!

But—there is a condition to having victory over the sin nature. That condition is to live under grace, not law of any kind.

According to this Scripture, if the sin nature is dominating any area of our life, then we have gone back to some form of law to defeat the sin problem. For example, if a born-again believer is struggling with a sin such as alcohol and repeatedly fails and repents, saying, "I will stop drinking; I can beat this thing," then they are looking to self. Their faith has moved to self instead of the cross where sin was defeated. No law or program of man, not even our own willpower will ever set us free from the sin that so easily besets us.

If the Christian tries to get victory over the sin nature by going to an encounter group or by entering a program or system of man, then they are putting themselves *under* law. The law is the strength of sin (I Cor. 15:56). They have not died to law but are fighting the sin nature by a law instead of fighting the good fight of faith. A twelve-step program or twenty-one days of fasting is not the answer for victory over sin as thousands of Christians have been falsely told.

These programs and systems of man become laws and will only strengthen the sin nature. We must not say no to sin but say yes to Jesus Christ and Him crucified! The cross is where sin was defeated. The cross is not just for salvation but for every need of the Christian. The sin nature shall not have dominion over you.

How to live for God in plain language:
By reckoning yourself to be dead to the sin nature, but alive to God in Christ Jesus our Lord!

HOW TO LIVE FOR
GOD
in plain language...

CHAPTER 10

NO CONDEMNATION

CHAPTER TEN
NO CONDEMNATION

"There is therefore now no condemnation to those who are in Christ Jesus, who do not walk according to the flesh, but according to the Spirit" (Rom. 8:1).

No condemnation, no guilty verdict. Thank You, Jesus, that by grace through faith we have been declared innocent of all charges!

This letter to the church in Rome was not broken into chapters and verses by the author, the Holy Spirit, or by the apostle Paul. The word *therefore* shows us it is a continuation of Paul's wretched man moment where he cried out, "Who will deliver me?" The answer came and immediately he gave thanks to *"God—through Jesus Christ our Lord!"* (Rom. 7:25). But now he knows that he is not condemned, eternally lost, every time he sins. Why? Because he is in Christ! We need to believe the Word of God and learn from the Scriptures that we are in Christ. This is our position. We are not condemned, nor do we lose our position in Christ every time we sin. In the mind of God, we were in Christ on the cross when He died, buried with Him, and rose from the dead with Him. Now, we are seated with Him *"in heavenly places in Christ Jesus"* (Eph. 2:5-6). This is our position, glory to God! As long as our faith remains in the finished work of Jesus, we are walking in the Spirit and have the verdict from God the Father of no condemnation.

The Holy Spirit always points to Jesus Christ and Him crucified. We are walking in the Spirit as we keep our faith continuously in His sacrifice. The Holy Spirit will not point us to ourselves or to our own strength. He will always point us to the cross where we received the verdict of no condemnation.

Walking in the flesh is when we look to, and depend on, our own strength for victory over any sin or a need in our lives. You may have heard the statement, "He was in the flesh." This means that the believer moved their faith off of Jesus and tried to make something happen by their own willpower. When we move our faith to something other than the blood of Jesus, we make a mess of the situation.

The Holy Spirit will convict us of a wrong direction or a sin in our lives. However, condemnation does not come from God. God has already given us the verdict of no condemnation. As long as our faith remains in the cross of Christ, we are in Christ, and we have the verdict of no condemnation— even when we sin! God forbid that we should sin, but when we sin, we have an advocate with the Father, Jesus Christ the righteous (I John 2:1). When we sin, we do not lose our position!

We see in Galatians 5:20 that an outburst of wrath is a work of the flesh. An outburst of wrath is a sin. Let me use this example. You lose your temper and start yelling at your spouse, "What's wrong with you? I told you not to do that! I can't believe this!" While you are yelling at your spouse, you have a heart attack and die. You are sinning at the moment you die. Are you going to heaven? The answer is yes because your faith is still in Christ! You have already been declared not guilty by our heavenly Father because your faith is in the finished work of the cross. Jesus took that sin upon Him on the cross. God forbid that we should sin, but our position does not change when we sin. Our condition will not be up to our position until the day we are glorified.

> "The heart is deceitful above all things, and desperately wicked; Who can know it?" (Jer. 17:9).

There are sins of the heart that we do not even know about. If you send a person to hell for yelling at their spouse, you are not judging that person, you are not even judging their sin, you are judging the blood of Jesus! The blood of Jesus either washes away all sin, or it does not. God has spoken, a verdict that has been rendered—no condemnation to those that are in Christ. God does not change the verdict based on our performance. The verdict is based on our faith in the obedience of Jesus' death, even the death of the cross (Phil. 2:8). Thank You, Jesus!

Some of you are getting nervous, so let us be clear that we are not talking about a license to sin! In Galatians Chapter 5, beginning in verse 19, we see the works of the flesh which are sins. Continuing to verse 21, we will see that the Bible does not teach a license to sin.

> "Now the works of the flesh are evident, which are: adultery, fornication, uncleanness, lewdness, idolatry, sorcery, hatred, contentions, jealousies, outbursts of wrath, selfish ambitions, dissensions, heresies, envy, murders, drunkenness, revelries, and the like; of which I tell you beforehand, just as I also told you in time past, that those who practice [do] such things will not inherit the kingdom of God" (Gal. 5:19-21).

Notice the word *practice* in this verse. It means "to continue without repentance." If we practice sin, we will not inherit the kingdom of God. If we continue the outbursts of wrath without repentance, we will not inherit the kingdom of God. Faith in the cross of Christ is not a license to sin! The cross of Christ is the victory over sin.

Many Christians have lived under condemnation far too long! With our faith in Jesus Christ and Him crucified, God has already given us the verdict of no condemnation. The Christian is not condemned by God. Condemnation comes from man, and that man can be you! The apostle Paul was given this two thousand years ago, and the Holy Spirit used his testimony to show us that we have freedom and liberty in Christ. If our faith remains in the sacrifice of God's Son, then we have been given the verdict of not guilty!

How to live for God in plain language:
With no condemnation!

HOW TO LIVE FOR GOD

in plain language...

CHAPTER 11

THE LAW OF THE SPIRIT

CHAPTER ELEVEN
THE LAW OF THE SPIRIT

"For the law of the Spirit of life in Christ Jesus has made me free from the law of sin and death" (Rom. 8:2).

Here we see two very powerful laws of God. God is not like man who changes His laws. The laws of God will never change. Looking at the latter part of this verse first, we see that there is the law of sin and death. If you sin, you die! There is no getting around it. It is going to happen. It is like the law of gravity; it happens every time. If you let go of this book, it will fall to the ground. It is a law. The law of sin and death is the same. If we sin, we die!

"For the wages of sin is death..." (Rom. 6:23)

Our sin has brought us death. *"The soul who sins shall die"* (Ezek. 18:4). Sin is the problem, and the problem brings death, but glory to God, there is a more powerful law—the law of the Spirit of life, not death, in Christ Jesus! If we keep our faith in Christ and His finished work of the cross, we have life not death! It is a law of God. It is the law of the Holy Spirit. This is how to live for God, in Christ, by faith in His finished work of the cross!

> *"...but the gift of God is eternal life in Christ Jesus our Lord"* (Rom. 6:23).

Jesus said He came to give us life and life more abundantly (John 10:10). The born-again believer will not experience the abundant life that Jesus promised until we embrace His finished work of the cross for our everyday living. It is a law of the Holy Spirit that if we remain in Christ, then we are free from the law of sin and death. The Holy Spirit will not operate in any other manner. It is a law! As long as our faith is in Jesus Christ and Him crucified, we will remain free from the law of sin and death.

The Holy Spirit will not give us victory over sin through a system of man! When we move our faith to something other than the cross of Christ, the Holy Spirit cannot help us because we are no longer exhibiting faith in Christ. It is a law of God!

Each and every one of us desires to remain free from the law of sin and death. That can only be accomplished by faith in the finished work of Jesus.

CHAPTER ELEVEN THE LAW OF THE SPIRIT

> *"So when Jesus had received the sour wine, He said, 'It is finished!' And bowing His head, He gave up His spirit"* (John 19:30)

While on the cross, Jesus cried with a loud voice, "It is finished!" which, in the Greek, is *teleo*. In Jesus' time, there were three ways that this word *teleo* was used. The first use was when an employer sent his worker into the field to do a job and, upon completion, the worker would return to his master and announce, "Teleo"—the work is done!

The second use for teleo was as an accounting term. If a farmer did not have money to buy the tools or the seed to plant his field, he would go to the merchant and on credit get the things he needed. The farmer would then plant, harvest, and sell his crop. He would then take that money and pay the merchant. The merchant would stamp on his invoice, "Teleo"—paid in full!

The third way teleo was used, was on the Day of Atonement. Once a year, the high priest would stand in the temple and all the children of Israel would bring their sacrifices. The priest would then inspect the lamb by shaving it and looking for any spot or blemish. It had to be perfect; it was a type of Christ. When the priest determined that the lamb was an acceptable sacrifice, he would cry out, "Teleo!"

When Jesus cried out with a loud voice from the cross, He was saying, "The work is done! It's paid in full! You have found the perfect Lamb! Stop looking for something else!

Stop running to other things!" Everything you need is found in His sacrifice on the cross! That sacrifice is the only thing the Holy Spirit recognizes. It is a law!

Bear in mind that the priest never asked the person what sins they had committed. He only looked at the sacrifice! If the sacrifice was accepted, then they were accepted. It is the same today! What is your sacrifice? Are you in Christ? Is your faith exclusively in the sacrifice of God's Son? It is God's most powerful law. It is the law of the Spirit of life in Christ! This law has made us free from the law of sin and death!

When the Christian tries to sanctify himself by any means other than faith in the cross, he has taken himself out from under God's law of the Holy Spirit. He will be a miserable Christian with no freedom, no victory, and no life!

How to live for God in plain language:
By the law of the Spirit of life in Christ Jesus.

# HOW TO LIVE FOR GOD

in plain language...

CHAPTER 12

THE WILLFUL SIN

CHAPTER TWELVE
THE WILLFUL SIN

"For if we sin willfully after we have received the knowledge of the truth, there no longer remains a sacrifice for sins, but a certain fearful expectation of judgement, and fiery indignation which will devour the adversaries" (Heb. 10:26-27).

Let us begin this study by explaining what the willful sin is not. It is not the acts of sin that we premeditate and then go ahead and do. It is singular. It is *the* willful sin.

The Holy Spirit is addressing believers, those of us that have received the knowledge of the truth. We have received Christ and are children of God. Our sin has been washed in the blood of Jesus (John 1:12). Thank God, that even when we commit sin, the blood of Jesus cleanses us from all unrighteousness—as long as our faith remains in His sacrifice. However, we must not misunderstand what the Holy Spirit is saying in these all-important Scriptures. There is a sin, the willful sin, that if committed, there no longer remains a sacrifice for that sin but judgement that will devour us.

What is the willful sin? If we take our faith off the finished work of Jesus, where all sin was atoned for, then we have committed the willful sin. If we move our faith off the finished work of Jesus, there no longer remains a sacrifice for our sin. Judgment and fiery indignation will devour us because we have now become an adversary *again*!

This blows another hole in the false doctrine of once saved always saved. You can lose your salvation! *"God… gave His only begotten Son, that whoever believes in Him should not perish but have everlasting life"* (John 3:16). Remember, He is writing to those who have already received the knowledge of the truth. He is talking to believers that no longer have faith in the sacrifice of God's Son.

In plain language: If we stop believing, then we have committed the willful sin and are no longer in the new covenant.

> *"Anyone who has rejected Moses' law dies without mercy on the testimony of two or three witnesses"* (Heb. 10:28)

It is not the person who breaks Moses' law, but rather the one who rejects Moses' law. He stops believing in the sacrifice provided! This does not happen suddenly to the Christian, but happens gradually, as we try to progressively sanctify ourselves. When the born-again believer tries to make himself righteous by looking to systems and programs of man instead of progressively being sanctified by faith in the cross, he is heading for disaster.

By trying every new sanctifying scheme of man that comes along, the believer will become unstable in all his ways and could eventually end up committing the willful sin. We are actually telling God, "I am adding this plan of man to your Son's sacrifice." It is unbelief!

Hebrews 10:28 is referring to Deuteronomy 17:2-3: *"If there is found among you, within any of your gates which the Lord your God gives you, a man or a woman who has been wicked in the sight of the Lord your God, in transgressing His covenant, who has gone and served other gods and worshiped them, either the sun or moon or any of the host of heaven, which I have not commanded."*

Transgressing the covenant is moving our faith to something else. Transgression is coming out from under the covenant and going another way. When we do this, we are no longer covered by the blood covenant. In verse 3, it tells us that they went and served other gods. When the believer today moves their faith off Jesus Christ and Him crucified, he has become a transgressor of the covenant. He does not believe anymore!

I personally know of several people that have transgressed the covenant and committed the willful sin. It has been very sad to see this happen. It did not happen overnight. Each person moved their faith little by little off the cross of Christ by trying this program and that system of man. They eventually lost their way.

"Of how much worse punishment, do you suppose, will he be thought worthy who has trampled the Son of God

> *underfoot, counted the blood of the covenant by which he was sanctified a common thing, and insulted the Spirit of grace"* (Heb. 10:29).

When a person stops believing in the cross of Christ, he is trampling the Son of God underfoot. He is regarding the blood of the covenant, which he was sanctified by, as a common, ordinary thing. This is the positional sanctification, which we *receive* at the time of our conversion.

The Word of God is not telling us that we lose our salvation when we foolishly try to progressively sanctify ourselves by law. It is not easy to lose our position in Christ, but it is possible! God will never leave us or forsake us, but we can leave Him.

Moving our faith off the sacrifice of God's Son for any need in our life starts us on a slippery slope. Eventually, this could lead us to take our faith off the blood of Jesus for our salvation. We would lose our positional sanctification because now we have committed the willful sin. We should heed this warning that we can insult the Holy Spirit and lose our way.

How do we live for God in plain language:

Our faith must be in the cross of Christ for us to be saved; this is *positional* sanctification. And our faith must remain in the cross of Christ throughout our Christian experience, which is *progressive* sanctification (Heb. 10:10,14). Amen!

HOW TO LIVE FOR GOD
in plain language...

CHAPTER 13

SANCTIFIED AND PRESERVED BLAMELESS

CHAPTER THIRTEEN
SANCTIFIED AND PRESERVED BLAMELESS

I would like to begin this chapter by making a statement that came to me after many trials, tribulations, and failures. We cannot, and we never will be able to, sanctify ourselves! Not positionally or progressively. We cannot make ourselves holy before or after we are saved by either what we do or do not do. We cannot sanctify ourselves!

The word *sanctification* in the Greek is *hagiasmos*. It means "separation unto God, to purify, to make holy continuously." Hagiasmos comes from the root word *hagiazo*, which means "to sanctify." And here is the problem—we Christians think that by doing good things, we can progressively sanctify ourselves. We actually "practice" sanctification by works, but we would never say it that way. We think that reading a certain number of chapters of the Bible a day makes us more holy. Or praying and fasting will sanctify us and make us more acceptable to God. Nothing could be further from the truth! Nothing can make us more holy than when the blood of Jesus was applied to our lives at the time of our salvation.

When we get saved, we are sanctified by faith in Jesus Christ and Him crucified. That is our position. This is a one-time positional sanctification experience. Faith is the only thing that pleases the Father. *"But without faith it is impossible to please Him"* (Heb. 11:6). However, that faith must have a very specific object. We are holy and righteous by faith in the sacrifice of God's Son. That alone and nothing else! The moment we took our faith off of religion, off of ourselves and put our faith on Jesus Christ and Him Crucified, we were declared holy by a holy God. That was the moment we were separated unto God and positionally sanctified. At that same moment, we begin the lifelong Christian walk and immediately enter into the progressive sanctification process.

> *"For by one offering He has perfected forever those who are being sanctified"* (Heb. 10:14).

The Bible calls it being sanctified, a continuous process of being made holy. It is an ongoing process in the life of a Christian. The first thing many Christians think is, "Are you saying that we don't need to read our Bibles, pray, fast, or do any other Christian disciplines?" Of course not! Do not fall for that foolish, simple-minded argument! Even the apostle Paul had to deal with religious men who were using that same argument. These men were trying to progressively sanctify themselves by works. We should pray and study the Word of God every day but not for righteousness and not to sanctify ourselves. Only our faith in Jesus' finished work of the cross continuously sanctifies us. It is the same specific object of faith in the sacrifice of God's Son, that both saves and continuously sanctifies the Christian.

> *"Now may the God of peace Himself sanctify you completely; and may your whole spirit, soul, and body be preserved blameless at the coming of our Lord Jesus Christ. He who calls you is faithful, who also will do it"* (I Thess. 5:23-24).

He will do what? Sanctify us! He makes us holy continuously. He sets us apart. He gives us peace because He is the God of peace. He preserves us as blameless and holy, a *continuous process,* until the coming of our Lord Jesus Christ. What an incredible truth! God sets us apart and keeps us holy until that day the Lord returns. Glory to God! Thank You, Jesus! Our faith in the sacrifice of God's Son, and nothing else, makes us holy and progressively sanctifies us. We are to rest in the finished work of Jesus and let the God of peace Himself sanctify us!

Paul is writing to the church of Thessalonica and, of course, to us believers today. The problem with today's church is that it is trying to sanctify itself in many different ways.

These new ways turn into laws and actually have the opposite effect. They bring the believer into captivity. The Christian becomes bound by works which grieves the Holy Spirit. The Holy Spirit does not lead us to perform an unbiblical plan of man that points to ourselves to be sanctified. God Himself sanctifies us completely! In plain language, running to these man-made ways of sanctification is unbelief! Do we really believe what Jesus said on the cross, "It is finished"?

> *"Speak also to the children of Israel, saying; 'Surely My Sabbaths you shall keep, for it is a sign between Me and you throughout your generations, that you may know that I am the Lord who sanctifies you. You shall keep the Sabbath, therefore, for it is holy to you. Everyone who profanes it shall surely be put to death; for whoever does any work on it, that person shall be cut off from among his people"* (Ex. 31:13-14).

We see here that that the sanctification process has never changed! So, who sanctifies us? The Lord sanctifies us! Jesus is our Sabbath rest! With our faith in His sacrifice on the cross, we are being sanctified by the Lord Himself. We are not made holy and set apart by any means other than faith in the finished work of the cross. In verse 14, the Scripture warns that we must not add any work to the finished work of Jesus. If we add our works to the cross of Jesus, we profane His sacrifice by which we are sanctified.

CHAPTER THIRTEEN SANCTIFIED AND PRESERVED BLAMELESS | 113

The Holy Spirit, knowing that the heart of man is deceitfully wicked and loves to perform works to sanctify himself, had James write, *"But someone will say, 'You have faith, and I have works.' Show me your faith without your works, and I will show you my faith by my works. You believe that there is one God. You do well. Even the demons believe—and tremble! But do you want to know, O foolish man, that faith without works is dead?"* (James 2:18-20).

What a truth! Faith without works is dead! Proper faith in the shed blood of the Lamb will produce proper works. I want to make this clear as to what the Holy Spirit through James was bringing out. Faith always comes first, then works will follow. Not the other way around! Abraham would show us his faith by his works. Abraham believed God (faith) and because of that faith, he took his son Isaac up on the mountain to sacrifice (works).

Helping to build a church in a third world country may be something that God has called some to do. However, if that person's faith is in that work to please the Father instead of in the cross of Christ, then he is trying to progressively sanctify himself. When the believer thinks he can progressively sanctify himself, he becomes self-righteous!

The same one trying to make himself holy by what he does, instead of simple faith in the sacrifice of God's Son, is the last one to know he is self-righteous! That man has his works ahead of his faith. *"God resists the proud, but gives grace to the humble"* (James 4:6). He is frustrating the grace of God! Faith must always come first and then the works will follow.

We must be careful that the object of our faith is the cross of Christ and not our works!

The word *sanctification* also has a dual meaning—to be separated unto God but also to be separated from the world, sin, and the law. Amen. But how? By my own willpower? By a law devised by men? Separated by gritting my teeth and gutting it out for God? No! No! No! In our own strength, we *cannot* separate ourselves unto God. Only the Holy Spirit can separate us unto a Holy God. When the Holy Spirit tells us to separate from something, He also empowers us by pointing us to the finished work of Jesus.

My own testimony is this: Before I was saved, I was shooting pool in a big tournament and won the championship that year. By the grace of God, a short time later, I was born again. The following year, I received an invitation to come back and defend my title. That night, I once again won the Northern New York 9 Ball Championship. I received the trophy and a cash prize. The news people were there and took my picture for the paper. As I drove away, I heard the Holy Spirit say, "I was not in that." I knew exactly what He meant. He did not save me to play pool. That night, I laid my pool stick down and have not played in another tournament for more than twenty years. It was a blessing to obey God! The bottom line is, faith in the blood of Jesus gave me the power to obey (I Cor. 1:18).

I did not sanctify or set myself apart from shooting pool. It was not of my own doing. It was not my idea. It was not a denominational rule or law that caused me to quit playing pool.

I did not progressively sanctify myself, set myself apart, the Holy Spirit did! When we make a law for ourselves, or someone makes a law for us to separate us unto God, we become very miserable Christians. If a pastor or religious system had told me I was not to shoot pool, it would have put me under law and strengthened my sin nature (I Cor. 15:56).

By faith in the cross, the believer is continuously set apart *for* God but also set apart *by* God! It was the Holy Spirit Himself who set me apart from something He did not want in my life. I want you to understand that shooting pool for you may be fine. He set me apart from playing pool, not you. It is not meant to be a law to be holy for anyone else. But for me, to shoot pool is a sin.

Religion is man trying to please God by what he does or does not do instead of placing his faith in what Jesus did for us on the cross. The sanctification process is by faith in the finished work of Christ. The sanctification process for believers has always been the same. There is no other way to be continuously made holy before a holy God.

If you are reading this right now, and the Holy Spirit has shown you areas of your life where you are trying to sanctify yourself, simply repent and ask God to forgive you and put your faith solely and completely in the cross of Christ.

How to live for God in plain language?
Say, "Thank You, Jesus, for Your shed blood on the cross that saves and sanctifies me!" Enter the sanctification process by faith alone! And rest!

HOW TO LIVE FOR GOD
in plain language...

CHAPTER 14

SANCTIFIED BY FAITH IN ME

CHAPTER FOURTEEN
SANCTIFIED BY FAITH IN ME

THE WORDS OF JESUS

Many of you know the story of the apostle Paul's conversion on the road to Damascus. This is the man God would use to write more than half of the New Testament. We will read Paul's testimony and then look at the Great Commission that Jesus Himself gave the apostle.

> *"While thus occupied, as I journeyed to Damascus with authority and commission from the chief priests, at midday, O king, along the road I saw a light from heaven, brighter than the sun, shining around me and those who journeyed with me. And when we all had fallen to the ground, I heard a voice speaking to me and saying in the Hebrew language, 'Saul, Saul, why are you persecuting Me? It is hard for you to kick against the goads'"* (Acts 26:12-14).

The chief priests had commissioned Saul (Paul) to stop the followers of Jesus from proclaiming Him to be the Messiah because many were becoming believers. Paul here is now testifying to King Agrippa of what he experienced on the road to Damascus. He saw a bright light, brighter than the sun. It was Jesus! The Light of the world!

Saul—Paul's name before his conversion—describes how he fell to the ground in the presence of Jesus. Paul, who was persecuting believers because of their faith, did not realize that he was actually persecuting Jesus Himself. The goads that Jesus spoke of were spikes on the front of a horse drawn wagon to keep the horse from kicking and destroying the wagon. When someone fights Jesus, like the apostle Paul did before his conversion, they are only hurting and destroying themselves. They are kicking against the goads!

> "So I said, 'Who are You, Lord?' And He said, 'I am Jesus, whom you are persecuting. But rise and stand on your feet; for I have appeared to you for this purpose, to make you a minister and a witness both of the things which you have seen and of the things which I will yet reveal to you. I will deliver you from the Jewish people, as well as from the Gentiles, to whom I now send you'" (Acts 26:15-17).

Notice the apostle Paul calls Him "Lord." Paul knows he is in the presence of God! Jesus answers, "I am Jesus," identifying

CHAPTER FOURTEEN SANCTIFIED BY FAITH IN ME | 121

Himself to Paul, just as He did at my conversion and every other believer's.

Jesus then tells Paul to stand up, for he is to receive instructions of where to go, what to preach and to whom. What a moment! Jesus Himself is going to begin to reveal the meaning of the new covenant to this brand-new Christian whom He will use to change the world! What does Jesus want Paul to preach to the Gentiles? The next verse tells us.

> *"To open their eyes, in order to turn them from darkness to light, and from the power of Satan to God, that they may receive forgiveness of sins and an inheritance among those who are sanctified by faith in Me"* (Acts 26:18).

The key word that I want us to see in the giving of this great commission is the word *and*. Jesus tells Paul what to preach—forgiveness of sins by faith in Me *and* an inheritance among those who are sanctified by faith in Me—two messages! Glory to God! *Justification* and *sanctification* by faith in Jesus! He did not leave us to progressively sanctify ourselves, which is impossible!

Now that our sins are forgiven by faith in Christ, we then also inherit sanctification by faith in Christ. You cannot earn or pay for an inheritance. You simply receive an inheritance. Jesus said we inherit sanctification "by faith in Me." We are continuously made holy and set apart by faith alone. That faith must be in Jesus' sacrifice and not in a foolish twelve or forty-day system devised by man. Faith in any of these other things deny the finished work of the cross.

Another condition needed to receive an inheritance is that someone has to die! That someone was Jesus! He died for our continuous sanctification. Glory! Glory! Glory to the Lamb forever!

He continuously makes us holy and separates us as we keep our faith in His finished work of the cross. This is liberty! This is freedom in Christ! This is the abundant life that Jesus promised!

We must stop trying to make ourselves acceptable to God by what we do or do not do. We are to believe that we are being sanctified, continuously made holy and separated unto God, by simple faith in Jesus. Of course, Jesus was not saying you do not have to do anything to be holy. To the contrary, He is telling the great apostle how to be holy and separated unto a holy God—"by faith in Me."

Many preachers are preaching the correct "what" to do. But without understanding the cross for sanctification, they are preaching the incorrect "how" to do it. Jesus is commissioning the apostle Paul to preach forgiveness of sins and how to live for God—"by faith in Me!"

In the following chapters of this book, you will see that once Paul received this great commission of sanctification by faith, he would preach and teach this message in all of his writings. The greatest message to the world is the first part of the commission that Jesus gave to Paul—forgiveness of sins *by faith in Me!* The greatest message to us, the church, is sanctification *by faith in Me!*

Can you imagine that moment on the road to Damascus when Paul had his encounter with Jesus? He would never be the same. He would never forget the words Jesus spoke to him. He may not have understood what it all meant, because Jesus said, *"the things which you have seen and of the things which I will yet reveal to you"* (Acts 26:16), but he would always remember what Jesus said. It is the same for us. We may not completely understand the message of the cross, but God is revealing it to us little by little. It is the sanctification process.

How to live for God in plain language:

Jesus said, "Sanctified by faith in Me."

HOW TO LIVE FOR GOD
in plain language...

CHAPTER 15

THE MESSAGE OF THE CROSS

CHAPTER FIFTEEN
THE MESSAGE OF THE CROSS

I would like for us to see in I Corinthians 1, that the problem the Holy Spirit was addressing in the church at Corinth was of true, born-again believers moving their faith off the cross of Jesus and instead looking to man for victory and power in their life. This is the same problem we are having in the church today.

> *"Paul, called to be an apostle of Jesus Christ through the will of God, and Sosthenes our brother, To the church of God which is at Corinth, to those who are sanctified in Christ Jesus, called to be saints, with all who in every place call on the name of Jesus Christ our Lord, both theirs and ours"* (I Cor. 1:1-2).

Around the world today, we have many calling themselves apostles. However, most are not God-called apostles.

Men such as these will always try to make followers of themselves instead of disciples of Christ. Their message is not Christ-centered and is dangerous for the Christians sitting under them. It is dividing the church today, just as it did in Corinth because the object of their faith moved from Christ and Him crucified to something else.

The Holy Spirit is using Paul to write a long letter to the true church of God, to all born-again believers that are sanctified in Christ Jesus. Paul begins by reminding the believer that they are sanctified, continuously made holy and set apart, by faith in Christ Jesus. Not by some program or system of man. Not by our works or a confession out of our mouth. Not through an encounter group or some other new fad of the modern church. But as Jesus said, *"sanctified by faith in Me"* (Acts 26:18).

This revelation of knowing that God is the sanctifier brings liberty and freedom. Some say it is like being born again—again! When the Christian receives the revelation of the cross for progressive sanctification and recognizes that he cannot sanctify himself, he is set free from works, law, and man's programs. We are to stand fast in the liberty by which Christ has made us free (Gal. 5:1). The Christian then understands that we do not have to perform for God to please Him. God is not looking at our performance to make us holy. He is looking at the focus of our faith.

Jesus told Paul on the Damascus road to preach "sanctification by faith in Me." We need to learn that faith in the

CHAPTER FIFTEEN THE MESSAGE OF THE CROSS | 129

finished work of Jesus is the one and only thing that gives the Holy Spirit the right to intervene in our lives. He will not glorify a man! Jesus said, when He [the Holy Spirit] comes *"He will glorify Me"* (John 16:14). We must clearly understand and believe what Jesus said. The Holy Spirit will glorify Me! When we move our faith off Jesus' finished work of the cross and look to the newest church scheme, we have removed the power source that allows the Holy Spirit to move in our lives.

You might be saying right now, "My faith is in the cross." Yes, all believers will rightly make that profession for salvation. However, where is your faith when it comes to the sanctification process? Most of the Bible is teaching us how to live for God, and the book of Corinthians is no exception.

Years ago, I shared the message of the cross for progressive sanctification with a pastor. His response was, "I'm not an evangelist. I'm not going to preach salvation every Sunday." He was only focused on the cross for salvation. I trust by now that you can see how close-minded even a man of God can be when it comes to the sanctification process. Man's default thinking of how to please God is, "What do I do?" The multitude came to Jesus and asked that very same question.

> *"Then they said to Him, 'What shall we do, that we may work the works of God?' Jesus answered and said to them, 'This is the work of God, that you believe in Him whom He sent'"* (John 6:28-29).

Believing in the finished work of Jesus is our work! The Greek word for work is *ergon,* which is a noun. It means "what you are occupied with, what it is your occupation." It is like a plumber, that is his occupation, that is his work. We are believers! Our work is to believe!

The Greek word for labor is *kopos,* a verb. It means "to beat the breast, to spend energy, to exhaust oneself." Work and labor are two different things! Today, the plumber is changing a water line; that is his *labor.*

All over the world Christians are known as believers, and what do we believe? The international symbol of Christianity is the cross. We believe in what Jesus did on the cross. Our labor is to do what God has asked us to do for His kingdom. We must not put our faith in our labor! If we do, then we have moved our faith off the cross and on to what we are doing!

The Christian must come to the point that we believe as the Bible teaches in Hebrews 11:6, *"But without faith it is impossible to please Him* [God]." Nothing in my hands I bring, simply to the cross I cling!

> *"Grace to you and peace from God our Father and the Lord Jesus Christ"* (I Cor. 1:3).

Grace and peace only come one way. We will not grow in grace or have the peace that passes all understanding in our lives, until our faith is exclusively in Jesus Christ and Him crucified. If you are not experiencing the peace that you once had at conversion, then you are not living under grace. You are not letting God Himself sanctify you. Once again, remember what Jesus said, *"Sanctified by faith in Me"* (Acts 26:18).

And that is why I am writing this book, *How To Live For God In Plain Language*. It is a call to the believer to come back to faith in the cross alone! To stop trying to progressively sanctify yourself as I tried so many years ago to do. We are to fight the good fight of faith! It is a good fight! We have the victory!

> *"Now I plead with you, brethren, by the name of our Lord Jesus Christ, that you all speak the same thing, and that there be no divisions among you, but that you be perfectly joined together in the same mind and in the same judgement. For it has been declared to me concerning you, my brethren, by those of Chloe's household, that there are contentions among you"* (I Cor. 1:10-11).

The Holy Spirit through the apostle is imploring believers that are saved and sanctified in Christ to speak one thing— Jesus Christ and Him crucified! If we testify about the power in the blood of Jesus, rest in the finished work of the cross, and fellowship around the sacrifice of God's Son, then there will be no divisions among us.

In verse 11, we see Paul addressing contentions among the brethren. Why do contentions manifest? Because one brother's faith for progressive sanctification is in a man-made system, while another has his faith in the latest bestseller at the

Christian bookstore. These programs of man are not Christ-centered and will never sanctify the believer or bring unity to the body of Christ. In an attempt to make us holy, these programs actually become laws which strengthen the sin nature and cause us to lose our peace.

Ask yourself if the program you are using right now is truly cross-centered where the Christian's victory was won. Or does it point your faith back to what you do instead of what Jesus did? The only true unity in the body of Christ is the cross! We are unified by faith in the shed blood of the Lamb!

You might be offended right now, but let me remind us all that the gospel is an offense. So read on, push through the offense, and let the Word of God teach you how to live for God.

> *"Now I say this, that each of you says, 'I am of Paul,' or 'I am of Apollos,' or 'I am of Christ.' Is Christ divided? Was Paul crucified for you? Or were you baptized in the name of Paul?"* (I Cor. 1:12-13).

Or ... "I am of the Church of God," or the Assemblies of God, or Baptist, or Methodist, or Purpose-Driven, or G-12." Or "I am of Christ." The Holy Spirit takes us immediately to the only true unity, the crucified Christ! Your denomination was not crucified for you! No program of man hung on a cross for you! You were not baptized in the name of your pastor! The body of Christ is divided because of the moving of their faith off the finished work of Jesus and looking to their own special programs to sanctify themselves. We must never look to the wisdom of the words of man.

> *"For Christ did not send me to baptize, but to preach the gospel, not with wisdom of words, lest the cross of Christ should be made of none effect"* (I Cor. 1:17).

To the pastor that is reading this right now, I say, what are you preaching? Are you preaching the wisdom of words? Is the message centered on Jesus Christ and Him crucified or have you made the cross of none effect?

To the Christian, I ask, What messages are you listening to? Does it lift up Christ and build your faith in Him, or does it point to man with wisdom of words?

When we preach or listen to any message other than Jesus Christ and Him crucified, we are making the cross of Christ of none effect. We are then saying that the blood of Jesus is not enough to continuously sanctify us. We are trying to make ourselves holy by a means other than the blood shed on the cross. We have now lost the benefits of the cross for our everyday living.

Remember, this is written to the church at Corinth, to those that are sanctified in Christ Jesus. Paul is not talking about our initial salvation. We must see clearly that faith in anything other than the finished work of Jesus on the cross is the wisdom of words. The Holy Spirit is talking about man's wisdom.

You might say, "I'm only doing this program or going to this encounter group to strengthen my faith." Going to an encounter group to receive something from God is unbelief! These things are not strengthening your faith in the blood of Jesus, they are pointing you to what you do. Anything that is not faith in the cross of Jesus is the wisdom of words and points a man to himself as the power source instead of the blood of Jesus.

There is only one gospel! One day, we will see the Lamb of God slain before the foundation of the world, and we will testify.

> "And they overcame him by the blood of the Lamb and by the word of their testimony, and they did not love their lives to the death" (Rev. 12:11).

When we stand before a holy God and give our testimony, what will it be? We will proclaim that we overcame the devil by the blood of the Lamb and the word of our testimony.

What will be the word of our testimony? Will it be us telling God what we did? "Oh God, I was a missionary. I read the Bible every day. I completed a twelve-day program of man. I fasted for twenty-one days! I never missed church, and I prayed to You often." No! When we are standing before our heavenly Father, we will not testify about what we did. We will be testifying about what Jesus did! "I overcame the devil by the blood of the Lamb, and the word of my testimony." The word of your testimony will be, "Look what Jesus did! Jesus saved me! Jesus delivered me! Jesus healed my body! Jesus baptized me in the Holy Spirit! Jesus sanctified me! Jesus, Jesus, Jesus!" We will be testifying about what Jesus did! It is not about our little programs or wisdom of words. We will not be testifying about anything else except the cross of Christ where the victory was won!

Why? The rest of Revelation 12:11 states, because we learned to love not our lives unto the death. We need to die to self, die to the programs and systems of the world, die to the law, die to sin, die to the flesh—then we will live for God by faith alone. Are you dead yet? Stay dead to these things. It is a good death.

> *"For the message of the cross is foolishness to those who are perishing, but to us who are being saved it is the power of God"* (I Cor. 1:18).

What did the Holy Spirit mean by *"the message of the cross?"* He did not mean a wooden beam or an idol around our neck. No, He is saying, what Jesus did for us on the cross by shedding His blood is the power of God! That is where the devil was defeated. That is when the veil of the temple into the holy of holies ripped in two. That is when Jesus cried out with a loud voice, "It is finished!" Once again, let us understand, that this is written to the church, to those of us that are sanctified in Christ Jesus (I Cor. 1:2).

The cross is foolishness to those that do not believe and who are perishing. They think, "What does a man who died on a cross two thousand years ago have to do with me?" "But to us that are saved, it is the power of God!" Power to live this Christian life. There is power in the blood! Glory to God!

Faith in the cross for everyday living does not make us sinlessly perfect. However, if the Christian is not experiencing victory in their life, it is because they are not looking exclusively to the cross where everything was provided.

Psychology is not the answer. Psychology starts with the idea that man is good, but something went wrong, and we need to find what made you bad. The Bible teaches just the opposite, that there is none good; we are all born bad, and the only good one is Christ (Rom. 3:10).

There is no such thing as a "Christian psychologist." Christianity, faith in Christ alone, refutes psychology. The church has embraced humanistic psychology so much that it has forsaken God's way of victory, the cross. If another man could talk sin, depression, bitterness, or unforgiveness out of our lives in a "counseling session," then Jesus did not have to go to the cross.

Christian, put your faith back in the cross of Jesus where you were first saved and experience the abundant life that Jesus promised. This sounds very simple, but it is not that easy for us to do.

Just pray right now: "Father, in the name of Your Son, Jesus, I am sorry for trying to please You by my works and trying to sanctify myself. At this very moment, I am putting my faith only in the finished work of Jesus! Not only for my salvation but, from now on, for every need in my life. Thank You for sending Jesus to die for me, for being obedient unto death, even the death of the cross. Thank You, Lord, for sanctifying me with Your Son's precious blood and giving me the abundant life that only You can give. Help me to keep my faith focused on the cross. In Jesus' name I pray, amen. Glory to God! Somebody just got the victory!

How to live for God in plain language:
By the word of the cross.

HOW TO LIVE FOR GOD

in plain language...

CHAPTER 16

GOD'S WISDOM, THE CROSS

CHAPTER SIXTEEN

GOD'S WISDOM, THE CROSS

We will continue in I Corinthians Chapter 1. Remember, the apostle Paul is writing to the church, which is you and me. The difference between God's wisdom, which is the cross, and man's wisdom, is like night and day. I assume everyone reading this has their faith in Jesus Christ and Him crucified for salvation. In this chapter, the Holy Spirit will challenge all believers to decide who they will put their faith in to remain righteous and holy. God or man?

> *"For it is written: 'I will destroy the wisdom of the wise, and bring to nothing the understanding of the prudent"* (I Cor. 1:19).

God Himself will destroy man's wisdom. He is the Creator, and we are the creation. Imagine how it makes God feel when His people forsake the sacrifice of His only begotten Son and turn to man's wisdom for any need in their lives. He will destroy our wisdom! The Christian that turns to anything other than the cross of Christ is telling God that man's wisdom is wiser than His. You might think, "You're taking this a little too far." Read the verse again, and then ask God the Father what He thinks about the wisdom of poor, pathetic man.

> *"Where is the wise? Where is the scribe? Where is the disputer of this age? Has not God made foolish the wisdom of this world? For since, in the wisdom of God, the world through wisdom did not know God, it pleased God through the foolishness of the message preached to save those who believe"* (I Cor.1:20-21).

The unbeliever looks to his own wisdom out of ignorance, but we that are saved by the blood should know better. The world's foolishness holds no answer for the Christian.

In verse 21, the word *save* in the Greek is the verb, *sozo*. Besides to save (salvation), it means "to heal, to deliver, to restore; to encompass everything the child of God needs."

What must we believe in as believers? The message preached, the message of the cross. There is only one message throughout the Bible, the message of the cross. All doctrine is founded on the basis of the cross of Christ.

> *"For Jews request a sign, and Greeks seek after wisdom; But we preach Christ crucified, to the Jews a stumbling block and to the Greeks foolishness"* (I Cor. 1:22-23).

All of mankind is searching for the meaning of life, but as preachers, we preach! We do not send the believer to a psychologist. We do not look to a man. We do not send them to an encounter group. We do not point the believer to themselves. We preach! And we preach Christ! We do not preach the newest scheme of man in the bookstore. We preach Christ, and we preach Christ crucified! We preach the cross! We preach the blood! We point to the sacrifice of God's Son, and only the sacrifice of God's Son! Why? Next verse.

> *"But to those who are called, both Jews and Greeks, Christ the power of God and the wisdom of God"* (I Cor. 1:24).

"Christ the power of God and the wisdom of God." I feel the presence of God as I write this. Read the Word again: *"Christ the power of God and the wisdom of God."* Thank You, Jesus, for the cross! Our faith must remain in Christ crucified if we want wisdom in our lives. The cross is the wisdom and power of God for the Christian!

> *"Because the foolishness of God is wiser than men, and the weakness of God is stronger than men"* (I Cor. 1:25).

We must understand what the Holy Spirit is saying through the apostle. God's ways are wiser and stronger than man's ways. When we go to a man-made system, we are saying that the cross of Christ was not enough. But you might say, "I am just doing what a lot of other Christians are doing." Yes, but they also are denying the finished work of the cross as the only way for the believer to be progressively sanctified. Many turn to themselves and man's wisdom in ignorance, but the Word of God leaves us with no excuse! Paul had to repent of dependency upon self and learn to trust only in God's provision—the finished work of the cross— and so do we.

The only biblical way of victory for the believer is faith in Jesus Christ and Him crucified!

In the remainder of I Corinthians 1, the Holy Spirit continues to show us how inadequate we are when it comes to living for God. Man-made systems only glorify the flesh (I Cor. 1:29). How ashamed and embarrassed we will be when we stand before God, and these man-made programs are put up alongside the cross of Jesus! When will we realize that they do not work? The blood of Jesus always works!

> *"But of Him you are in Christ Jesus, who became for us wisdom from God—and righteousness and sanctification and redemption—that, as it is written, 'He who glories, let him glory in the Lord'"* (I Cor. 1:30-31).

We are in Christ Jesus. He is our everything! He is our sanctification! When we get to heaven, we will only be glorying in the Lord! So we need to start living right now with our faith firmly placed in the cross!

CHAPTER SIXTEEN **GOD'S WISDOM, THE CROSS** | **145**

Let us look at some of the key words and phrases that the apostle Paul uses in Chapter 1 of his letter to the church at Corinth:

The will of God	Cross of Christ
Power of God	Sanctified in Christ
Wisdom of words	Wisdom of God
Called to be saints	The Cross of none effect
No flesh will glory	Grace
Message of the cross	In Christ Jesus
Peace	Power of God
Righteousness	Blameless
Destroy wisdom of wise	Sanctification
No divisions	Foolishness
Redemption	I Am of Christ
Preach Christ crucified	Glory in the Lord

How to live for God in plain language:
By the message of the cross—it is the power of God!

THE STRENGTH OF SIN IS IN THE LAW

So, you turned to this page and looked ahead!

In Chapter 2, I gave you one "law" to show you the truth—that the law, any law, is the strength of the sin nature.

And if you are one of the few who did not look, good for you! However, you wanted to look ahead, because your sin nature was still strengthened!

It is the truth! *"The strength of sin is the law"* (I Cor. 15:56). It is the almighty Word of God!

The law, not grace, is the strength of the sin nature. Amen.

HOW TO LIVE FOR GOD

in plain language...

CHAPTER 17

JESUS CHRIST AND HIM CRUCIFIED

CHAPTER SEVENTEEN
JESUS CHRIST AND HIM CRUCIFIED

As we continue our study, we will look at I Corinthians 2:1-5. This is the apostle Paul's testimony to the church at Corinth and for us today. It started on the road to Damascus where he had an encounter with Jesus. He was saved and then instructed to preach forgiveness of sins and sanctification "by faith in Me." However, this revelation of sanctification "by faith in Me" did not come easy. It was years later, after many personal struggles with the sin nature overriding his willpower and dominating his life that he could then write with authority from the Holy Spirit how to live for God.

By the time he wrote the letter to the Corinthians, he had determined to know nothing except Jesus Christ and Him crucified. I am trusting that as we go through these five verses, each of you will also make up your own mind to look only to the sacrifice of the Son of God.

> *"And I, brethren, when I came to you, did not come with excellence of speech or of wisdom declaring to you the testimony of God"* (I Cor. 2:1).

Paul is speaking to the brethren at the church in Corinth that he had established years earlier. The Holy Spirit is of course also addressing all of us believers today. God knew we would be reading this, even this very day. The Holy Spirit is telling us that it is not excellent speech or man's wisdom we need. What we need is far more powerful. We need the wisdom of God, which is the cross.

> *"For I determined not to know anything among you except Jesus Christ and Him crucified"* (I Cor. 2:2).

Like Paul, each of us must determine—make up our mind— not to know anything except Jesus Christ and His finished work of His cross! Why the cross? That is where Jesus won the victory! Victory in every area of the believer's life. Jesus Christ is the source, and the cross is the means by which God chose to give us life. That has been the plan of God from before the foundation of the world, the Lamb slain! *"Without shedding of blood there is no remission"* (Heb. 9:22). The cross is the answer before we are saved, and the cross is the answer *after* we are saved. The cross is the answer for the Christian as well as the unbeliever. Nothing else. Only the blood! The finished work of Jesus on the cross is the only answer for sin.

CHAPTER SEVENTEEN JESUS CHRIST AND HIM CRUCIFIED

When us Christians begin to struggle with sin, any sin, we must not try to fight the thing in our own strength. The church world runs after programs of man like the purpose-driven, twelve steps, encounter groups, etc. But the Bible teaches to look to Jesus and His finished work. The blood never loses its power! Stop fighting sin and start fighting the fight of faith. Determine to know nothing else except Jesus Christ and Him crucified.

Because of His foreknowledge, God knew He would have to save us from our sin. He also wanted us to have an abundant life on this earth before we make heaven our home. His provision is the sacrifice of His Son for both our salvation and the abundant life.

You might be asking right now why the Holy Spirit is not mentioning the resurrection. When the Bible talks about the cross, it is with the understanding that of course Jesus rose from the dead and is alive. We cannot separate the finished work of the cross from the resurrection, but we must have them in their proper place.

Brother Swaggart says it plain, "The resurrection was dependent on the cross, the cross was not dependent on the resurrection." No man took His life; He gave it freely (John 10:18). He could have come off the cross, but He stayed there for you and for me!

Jesus said He would be in the belly of the earth for three days and three nights, just as Jonah was three days and three nights in the belly of the fish (Matt.12:40). Jesus said He would rise from the dead, so the resurrection was going to happen! But in the garden, just before He went to the cross, he prayed to His Father.

> "O My Father, if it is possible, let this cup pass from Me; nevertheless, not as I will, but as You will" (Matt. 26:39).

What was the will of the Father for His Son? To go to the cross and shed His blood for you and for me. The cross is where the victory was won, not at the resurrection!

> "And declared to be the Son of God with power according to the Spirit of holiness, by the resurrection from the dead" (Rom. 1:4).

The resurrection declared Him to be the Son of God with power. The resurrection makes the statement; Jesus never sinned but paid for all of our sins. If even one of our sins had not been paid for, then Jesus could not have been raised from the dead. The Spirit of holiness has declared it. Glory to God! And because He lives, I live also!

With this knowledge, we can now focus our faith exclusively on Jesus Christ and Him crucified. It was on the cross that Jesus shed His blood. It was from the cross that Jesus proclaimed with a loud voice, "It is finished," not after the resurrection.

As we read the Bible through the knowledge of the finished work of the cross, the power of God is revealed to us.

Glory to God! We can now have abundant life! No, we are not sinlessly perfect, but we now know where to go when we have a need in our life—the cross!

Thank You, Father, for sending your Son, who was *"obedient to the point of death, even the death of the cross"* (Phil. 2:8). Thank You, Lord, for my salvation, my sanctification, my healings, my deliverance, and the baptism in the Holy Spirit. Thank you for the liberty I have in Jesus! I love You, Lord! I have determined not to know anything except Your Son's finished work of the cross. His victory is now my victory!

> *"I was with you in weakness, in fear, and in much trembling"* (I Cor. 2:3).

We must all make up our minds to *put away* the wisdom of man and look only to the cross of Christ! The Holy Spirit admonishes us throughout God's Word to not put our faith in man but to keep our faith in the crucified Christ. This is a problem for many Christians. The pride of man causes us to not want to put certain things out of our lives. After all, what could be wrong with the Word of Faith system that man came up with? Simply put, it has the wrong object of faith.

The Word of Faith "program" that we see being taught today, is not God's designated way of victory for the Christian. This program of man teaches one to put their faith in what they say or do not say, do or not do. In the Lord's Prayer, even Jesus Himself said, "Your kingdom come, Your will be done."

This so-called Word of Faith system is not Christ-centered! Many would fight me on that statement because they have not determined to know nothing else except Jesus Christ and Him crucified. Their faith is still in themselves. We need to continue to pray for our brothers and sisters that are trapped in this false way.

> *"God resists the proud, but gives grace to the humble"* (James 4:6).

Naming and claiming things is not humility. It is self-centered, not Christ-centered. It is the pride of man! The word *resists* means "to set an array of armies around you." God's army! When we become prideful, God will have His army set against us. Our faith should not be in our self or what we say, which lifts man up with pride. God forbid! Our faith is to be the *"faith of the Son of God"* (Gal. 2:20). A man or woman that walks around declaring this or claiming that has not been crucified with Christ (Gal. 2:20). They are boasting in themselves (Gal. 6:14). They have not denied self and determined to know nothing else save Jesus Christ and Him crucified (Luke 9:23, I Cor. 2:2).

Jesus said, *"Assuredly, I say to you, unless you are converted and become as little children, you will by no means enter the kingdom of heaven"* (Matt. 18:3).

I want us to understand what Jesus was saying, when he said, *"become as little children."* When we are converted and born again, we are new creations in Christ Jesus. This is the beginning of a new life. Now that we are born again, we must become as little children. It is a process of learning dependency on God.

When we are born into this life on earth, we are totally dependent on our mother. As we begin to mature, we start to become independent. At a year old, we walk; we are more independent. At two years old, we talk; more independent. At sixteen, we drive a car. At twenty, we move out of the house and get married. We are maturing and becoming more and more independent.

But with God, it is just the opposite! When we are born again, we must learn to become as little children. Maturity in Christ is learning to become more and more dependent on Him. To grow in the grace and knowledge of Him, we must progressively become as little children. This is the weakness the Holy Spirit is talking about in verse 3. *"For when I am weak, then I am strong"* (II Cor. 12:10).

> *"And my speech and my preaching were not with persuasive words of human wisdom, but in demonstration of the Spirit and of power"* (I Cor. 2:4).

The only way a believer will experience the demonstration of the Holy Spirit is when they determine to know nothing except Jesus Christ and Him crucified. We must keep our faith there and only there! Just like Paul, preachers must determine to preach only the cross of Christ for every need of the believer. Then and only then will we experience the power of God in our lives through the moving and operation of the Holy Spirit.

> *"That your faith should not be in the wisdom of men but in the power of God"* (I Cor. 2:5).

We must examine ourselves to see if we are in the faith! (II Cor. 13:5). Is your faith exclusively in the sacrifice of God's Son, or is there something else you are looking to? What is in your library right now? Who are you listening to on the radio or watching on television? Are they preaching Jesus Christ and Him crucified? Faith in anything other than the cross of Christ is the wisdom of men. Let me say it one more time. The Word of God says that our faith must be in Jesus Christ and Him crucified, or we cannot please the Father (Heb. 11:6). Our faith must be in the power of God. What is the power of God? The message of the cross is the power of God (I Cor. 1:18).

Christian, I ask you, is your faith in Jesus Christ and Him crucified and only in Jesus Christ and Him crucified?

How to live for God in plain language:
You must determine to know nothing else except Jesus Christ and Him crucified! Amen!

HOW TO LIVE FOR GOD
in plain language...

CHAPTER 18

POSITIONAL SANCTIFICATION

CHAPTER EIGHTEEN
POSITIONAL SANCTIFICATION

We were all born under law and condemned to die. When a person puts their faith in the sacrifice of God's Son to wash away their sin, they are instantly sanctified. Their position immediately changes from condemned to saved. Their new position is now in Christ. This is positional sanctification. They are sanctified by faith alone!

In Hebrews 10, the Holy Spirit proves and confirms that the ceremonial law, including the priesthood, has been fulfilled in Christ. The Bible says, *"For Christ is the end of the law for righteousness to everyone who believes"* (Rom. 10:4). The ceremonial law, as well as the Ten Commandments, were fulfilled by Christ. Jesus said, *"I did not come to destroy the law but to fulfill [the law]"* (Matt. 5:17).

The word *sanctify* in the Greek is *hagiazo*. It means "to make holy, to make clean, render pure, to consecrate, devote, set apart from a common to a sacred use." The Word of God is clear, we cannot sanctify ourselves. It is by faith alone!

Religious men use laws to try to make themselves holy. Question: If God does not use laws, not even the Ten Commandments to sanctify us, then why do men feel as though they can be sanctified by something that they do or do not do? Religious men have no part in God or His plan of salvation.

God gave the Ten Commandments to show us our sin and to bring us to Christ. The Ten Commandments would condemn us and show us that we need to put our faith in Jesus' finished work of the cross. Our faith alone in Jesus' finished work of the cross would make us holy and positionally sanctify us, not the law! The law had a purpose—to bring us to Christ. But the law had no power to make us holy.

If we put a sign on the lawn that says, "Do not walk on the grass," then someone is going to want to walk on the grass and break the law. The law is the strength of sin (I Cor. 15:56). When we try to sanctify and make ourselves acceptable to God with rules and regulations, then the power source is our willpower. Our willpower is no match for the sin nature.

> *"For the law, having a shadow of the good things to come, and not the very image of the things, can never with these same sacrifices, which they offer continually year by year, make those who approach perfect. For then would they not have ceased to be offered? For the worshipers, once purified, would have had no more consciousness of sins. But in those sacrifices there is a reminder of sins every year.*

CHAPTER EIGHTEEN POSITIONAL SANCTIFICATION

For it is not possible that the blood of bulls and goats could take away sins" (Heb. 10:1-4).

Primarily, the book of Hebrews is addressing the Jewish people. However, we know, that the Bible is written to all mankind, forever and always. In these four verses, the Bible clearly tells us that the sacrifices offered under the law, even the ceremonial laws of God, could never make us perfect. God cannot have sin in His presence, therefore, we cannot approach God because of our sin. The ceremonial law instructed the priest to shed the blood of innocent animals. That blood would cover but not remove their sins. It was a foreshadow of the good things to come. The good things to come, would be Jesus Christ and Him crucified, whose blood would remove their sins. The purpose of the law was to point us to Christ.

I am continually shocked and saddened as I see true, born-again believers going back to the shadow of the law. The blood of Jesus, that the shadow of the law pointed to, has already been shed on the cross over two thousand years ago. Why do some Christians want to return to the shadow when we have the finished work of the cross? Why do they need prayer cloths, replicas of the ark of the covenant to kneel around, and shofars to blow when God has already sent Jesus? Because they want to be like Israel? Let me remind them that Israel to this day has rejected the Messiah.

Unless we are perfect and without sin, we cannot approach God. Only the blood of Jesus can make us perfect.

The ceremonial sacrifices would have to be offered continually year by year and would only cover sin, not take sin away.

John the Baptist proclaimed, *"Behold! The Lamb of God who takes away the sin of the world"* (John 1:29).

> *"Therefore, when He came into the world, He said: 'Sacrifice and offering You did not desire, But a body You have prepared for Me"* (Heb. 10:5).

When we read these next few verses, the Holy Spirit is recounting a conversation between Jesus and the Father. We may substitute Jesus for "He" and the Father for "You." Jesus was speaking to the Father. Again, this is undeniable proof that, *"There are three that bear witness in heaven: the Father, the Word, and the Holy Spirit; and these three are one"* (I John 5:7).

In this verse, Jesus said the Father did not desire sacrifice and offerings. The sacrifice and offerings were only to point sinful man to the Lamb of God—to Jesus Himself! Jesus goes on to say that the Father had prepared a body for Him. This would be the body that would be offered on the cross. God is Spirit and cannot die. So God would have to become a man to pay the price for man's sin.

Man sinned in the garden and therefore sin passed to all men. So, *"all have sinned and fall short of the glory of God"* (Rom. 3:23). It would take a man—the Man, Christ Jesus—to pay for our sin. *"Without the shedding of blood there is no remission [of sin]"* (Hebrews 9:22).

Jesus is proclaiming that the Father had prepared an earthly body for Him so He could become the sacrifice that would positionally sanctify all who would believe. The believer receives this one-time declaration by God of perfection at the time of their conversion.

> "In burnt offerings and sacrifices for sin You had no pleasure" (Heb. 10:6).

How can Jesus say that the Father had no pleasure in the burnt offerings and sacrifices for sin? For it was God the Father who gave us the ceremonial law and told man to offer sacrifices to atone for, but not take away, sins. But yet God had no pleasure in the actual sacrifice of the animal. God only had pleasure in what the sacrifices represented—Jesus Christ and Him crucified! Please, we must understand this very important point. In plain language, God had no pleasure in a man taking a knife and cutting the throat of an innocent lamb so the hot blood would pour out. He only had pleasure in what the sacrifice represented!

Our faith in His Son's sacrifice on the cross is the only way to please the Father!

Man must understand that by going to church, helping to build an orphanage in a third world country, or mowing the elderly lady's lawn next door does not make him acceptable before a holy God. Doing these things does not sanctify us! Nothing we physically do—not even the sacrificing of an innocent animal under the old covenant—could please the Father. His pleasure is when our faith is in the sacrifice of His Son, and nothing else.

Millions of animals died under the old covenant and could never make man perfect. God's standard is perfection. We must put our faith in what Jesus did on the cross to please the Father. Let me be clear. Going to a prayer meeting every week does not please the Father! Of course we should go to prayer meetings, but not to please Him. Only faith in the finished work of Jesus on the cross pleases the Father (Heb. 11:6). What is your faith in?

> *"Then I said, 'Behold, I have come—in the volume of the book it is written of Me'"* (Heb. 10:7).

Here, Jesus is speaking to the Father and says the Bible is written about Himself. From Genesis to Revelation, the Word of God speaks about the sacrifice of God's Son. It speaks about Jesus and Him crucified. We, as believers, need to look for the scarlet cord, which runs throughout the Bible. In every book of the Bible, and in every chapter, we can find the cross of Christ. The types and shadows in the Old Testament are clearly explained in the New Testament. Jesus says, *"To do Your will, O God"* (Heb. 10:9). What was the will of the Father for the Son? To go to the cross! To shed His precious blood for our sins! Thank God that Jesus was *"obedient to the point of death, even the death of the cross,"* so we could be sanctified

(Phil. 2:8). We must never return to the types and shadows. Our heavenly Father has provided His very best! His Son!

> *"Previously saying, 'Sacrifice and offering, burnt offerings, and offerings for sin You did not desire, nor had pleasure in them' (which are offered according to the law), then He said, 'Behold I have come to do Your will, O God.' He takes away the first that He may establish the second"* (Heb. 10:8-9).

The Holy Spirit through the apostle repeats Himself, so there is no mistaking that the old covenant was for a period of time. That time is over. God took away the old covenant to establish a new and better covenant, which has better promises (Heb. 8:6). Notice what He adds in Hebrews 10:8, *"which are offered according to the law."* Christ has fulfilled the law (Matt. 5:17).

> *"For the law was given through Moses, but grace and truth came by Jesus Christ"* (John 1:17).

The law was given, but grace and truth came by Jesus! Came! Jesus came for us! Thank You, Father, for sending Your Son, Jesus, who came and was obedient to do the will of God, fulfilling the law to establish grace! You took away the old covenant to establish the new covenant! You took away the law to establish grace! Glory to Your name!

> *"By that will we have been sanctified through the offering of the body of Jesus Christ once for all"* (Heb. 10:10)

By "that," meaning the sacrifice of the cross, we are positionally sanctified. This is the Christian's position. This is who we are! We are holy, clean, pure, set apart from a common thing to a sacred thing. By the onetime offering of the body of Jesus Christ and our faith in "that" sacrifice. Nothing else sanctifies us! It is a onetime and forever positional sanctification we receive the moment we place our faith in the sacrifice of God's Son. That was the will of the Father. We must never move our faith off the only thing that pleases the Father, Jesus Christ and Him crucified.

> *"And raised us up together, and made us sit together in heavenly places in Christ Jesus"* (Eph. 2:6).

What is our position? Seated together in Christ!

How to live for God in plain language:
Positionally sanctified by faith in the cross of Christ. Amen!

HOW TO LIVE FOR GOD
in plain language...

CHAPTER 19

PROGRESSIVE SANCTIFICATION

CHAPTER NINETEEN
PROGRESSIVE SANCTIFICATION

In the previous chapter, we learned that we are positionally sanctified, made holy by simple faith in the onetime sacrifice of God's Son on the cross. There is nothing we can do to save or make ourselves holy and righteous before a holy God. We simply put our faith in the finished work of the perfect one, Jesus Christ. We cannot set ourselves apart or change ourselves from a common thing to a sacred thing. If that were possible, then Jesus did not have to come and give His life for us. But with faith in the blood He shed on the cross, we are holy and blameless before God. This is our position. Washed in the blood!

Please notice that the Holy Spirit did not mention the resurrection regarding our sanctification. He is not diminishing the significance of the resurrection of Jesus from the dead but teaching us that the victory over sin was won on the cross! Thank God Jesus was raised from the dead, it is the first fruits of our resurrection. However, it was on the cross that the veil of the temple was ripped in two. It was on the cross that Jesus cried with a loud voice, "It is finished!" No man took His life; He gave it freely (John 10:18).

As we continue Hebrews 10, we will learn that the same way we were positionally sanctified, by grace through faith in Christ, is the same way we are being sanctified. This being sanctified, or progressive sanctification, is an ongoing process for all Christians. Progressive sanctification is not carried out by our own efforts but rather by the Holy Spirit as we keep our faith in the finished work of Jesus. Just as we could not initially or positionally sanctify and make ourselves acceptable to a holy God by what we did before faith in Christ, we also cannot progressively sanctify ourselves now that we are saved.

We were positionally sanctified by grace through faith in the sacrifice of God's Son. Now God progressively sanctifies us, by grace through faith in the cross! The Bible says that God Himself continuously sanctifies the believer as we exhibit faith in the finished work of Jesus, His Son.

> *"Now may the God of peace Himself sanctify you completely; and may your whole spirit, soul, and body be preserved blameless at the coming of our Lord Jesus Christ"* (I Thess. 5:23).

Who makes us holy and sets us apart? God! God sanctifies us completely! Complete in Christ! Nothing left to do to make us holy. We cannot do it! God makes us holy! Complete holiness! We cannot continuously make ourselves holy and set apart for God by means of our own willpower or a man-made program of dos and don'ts. This is progressive sanctification. Wow! Think of this great truth! If we keep our faith in the cross of Jesus, the God of peace Himself will keep us and preserve us blameless until Jesus returns!

Thank God the cross was a finished work! Jesus said to the apostle Paul on the road to Damascus in Acts 26:18, preach forgiveness of sins "by faith in Me" and sanctified "by faith in Me." So, what is our part in the ongoing progressive sanctification process? To keep our faith in the cross of Christ! This is being obedient to the faith (Rom. 1:5).

> *"And every priest stands ministering daily and offering repeatedly the same sacrifices, which can never take away sins. But this Man, after He had offered one sacrifice for sins forever, sat down at the right hand of God, from that time waiting till His enemies are made His footstool"* (Heb. 10:11-13).

Under the old covenant, God instituted the priesthood. Under the new covenant, Jesus is now our high priest (Heb. 3:1). Under the old covenant, the priest would stand. Under the new covenant, Jesus sat down at the right hand of the Father. Jesus did not sit down because He was tired! He sat down because the work was finished! Under the old covenant, the priest had to offer the sacrifices repeatedly every day.

Under the new covenant, Jesus offered one sacrifice for sins forever! Under the old covenant, the sacrifices could never take away sins. Under the new covenant, it is *"the Lamb of God who takes away the sin of the world!"* (John 1:29).

We have a better covenant with better promises, the everlasting covenant. (Heb. 8:6) Thank You, Jesus!

We were once enemies of God. Unbelievers are His enemies that will become His footstool (Ps. 110:1).

Thank God that we are no longer His enemies. We have been adopted into the family of God by simple faith in the sacrifice of God's Son.

> *"For by one offering He has perfected forever those who are being sanctified"* (Heb. 10:14).

Back in Hebrews 10:1, we read that the ceremonial law of sacrificing innocent animals could never make perfect, holy, and righteous those who approached God. But now, in verse 14, we see that God has perfected, forever, those that are being sanctified.

The scholars that translated the New King James Version of the Bible from Greek to English correctly make the distinction between our initial positional sanctification in Hebrews 10:10, and our "being sanctified" in verse 14. We are being sanctified continuously made holy and set apart by God Himself every day by faith in the offering of the body of Jesus.

CHAPTER NINETEEN **PROGRESSIVE SANCTIFICATION** | 173

There is freedom in the cross of Christ! This takes the pressure off of us to perform for God. This is the liberty we have in Christ, who has fulfilled the law for us. The cross of Christ is not a license to sin, God forbid! The blood of Jesus is the victory over sin! We are progressively sanctified and preserved blameless as we keep our faith exclusively in the sacrifice of God's Son. We are being sanctified!

All of the programs of man that have come our way in the last seventy-five years have been trying to progressively sanctify the believer. They are adding to the finished work of Jesus as if He did not say, "It is finished!"

The answer for depression is faith in the cross! The answer for deliverance from sin, Christian, is faith in the cross! Our healing comes through the blood! Whenever the Holy Spirit refers to the cross, He is talking about what Jesus did there. Do not think about a wooden beam with your carnal mind!

Let the Holy Spirit, who authored the Bible, quicken this great truth of continuous sanctification by faith in the sacrifice of God's only begotten Son!

Nowhere in the Bible does it tell us to fight against sin. The Holy Spirit tells us to fight the good fight of faith! (I Tim. 6:12). Why does He say fight? Because our flesh wants these programs and systems of man. Then, we can think we have a part in our sanctification process. Bottom line, it is pride! I can do it! I can make myself holy! I can set myself apart to God by doing this, and not doing that! No, we cannot!

We think if we read ten chapters of the Bible a day, or if we pray for one hour each morning, then we will be more holy before God. If I don't watch too much television or don't drink coffee, I will please God. No, these things do not sanctify, make holy, or set apart the believer. We are continuously sanctified by faith alone. Not faith in what I am doing—not even good Christian disciplines—but rather faith alone in what Jesus did on the cross!

When we try to sanctify ourselves, it will only bring condemnation because, eventually, we will fail in one area or another.

Under man-made laws, our power source is our own willpower. But with our faith in the finished work of Jesus, and only the finished work of the cross of Christ, the power source is the Holy Spirit. The Holy Spirit can now work within us to conform us into the image of Christ.

When we try to sanctify ourselves, we shut off the Holy Spirit as the power source. We must be Christ-centered, not man-centered because the Holy Spirit will not glorify a man. The Holy Spirit only works in our lives as our faith is in Jesus Christ and Him crucified!

The Holy Spirit forever points us to the victory Jesus won on the cross! When we yield to His leading, Christ's victory becomes our victory. Glory to God and the Lamb slain!

Some of you will bristle at this because you have your favorite man-made system. Remember, the Holy Spirit showed Paul this great truth and the apostle Paul testified,

"For I determined not to know anything among you except Jesus Christ and Him crucified" (I Cor. 2:2).

If you haven't already, make up your mind right now! Turn away from all of these other man-made things! Put your faith back in the cross of Christ for salvation and sanctification! It will be joy unspeakable and full of glory, just like the day you received Jesus as your Savior.

How to live for God in plain language:
By being progressively sanctified by faith in the finished work of Jesus on the cross!

# HOW TO LIVE FOR
GOD
in plain language…

CHAPTER 20

HOW TO WALK IN
THE SPIRIT

CHAPTER TWENTY
HOW TO WALK IN THE SPIRIT

The Word of God tells us that we can either walk after the flesh or after the Spirit. A believer does not want to walk after the flesh, which produces works of the flesh. If we are truly born again, we hate the works of the flesh. That is why we need to learn how to walk in the Spirit and therefore not fulfill the lust of the flesh.

We will find out from the Scriptures that the law, or the absence of law, once again plays a major role in our walk with the Lord. We will either live under grace exclusively, with our faith focused on the blood of Jesus, which produces the fruit of the Spirit, or we will add law to grace, which will strengthen the sin nature and produce the works of the flesh. We must not live under grace and at the same time practice law.

> *"Stand fast therefore in the liberty by which Christ has made us free, and do not be entangled again with a yoke of bondage"* (Gal. 5:1).

The Holy Spirit says through Paul, "stand fast!" If we keep our faith in the finished work of Jesus, we will have liberty. And grace will abound (Rom. 5:20). Faith in Christ has made us free from the law of sin and death (Rom. 8:2). It is the law of the Holy Spirit that when we are in Christ Jesus, we have life. In order to have this liberty, we need to stand fast with our faith in the cross. As we have stated before, whenever the Bible uses the word *cross*, it is always talking about what Jesus did on the cross.

In Galatians 5:1, the yoke of bondage refers to going back to law. Anything and everything we put our faith in that is not Jesus Christ and Him crucified becomes a yoke of bondage! "But wait a minute," I had one pastor tell me, "I received a lot of good things out of that purpose-driven book." It is a law because it is not Christ-centered. It is all about you and what you do each day. There is no liberty when we look to anything outside of the finished work of Jesus. The Holy Spirit calls it a "yoke of bondage." We are not living under grace alone when using a system of man. We have added law!

Man's default position is to go back to law for our daily needs. We like law because it means we get to do something. We think we can now sanctify ourselves. Jesus said from the cross, with a loud voice, "It is finished!" Believe it, live it, and stand fast in the liberty in which Christ has made you free! Do not go back to law!

> *"Indeed I, Paul, say to you that if you become circumcised, Christ will profit you nothing"* (Gal. 5:2).

CHAPTER TWENTY HOW TO WALK IN THE SPIRIT

The apostle Paul uses circumcision to represent the law, any law. The word *law* in the Greek is *nomos*—what one has in use and possession, a usage, custom or anything established by use. Meaning that the law can come from God or man. That man can be you! We make laws for ourselves for a variety of reasons—to defeat the sin nature, to please God, to look good in the eyes of our brothers and sisters, and the list goes on and on. If we go the way of law, Christ will profit you nothing!

If we are honest, each and every Christian has gone back to law at some point in their walk in an effort to please God. Now, with grace abounding and our faith focused on the sacrifice of God's Son, we have liberty and victory in our lives. We are not yoked to law, but we are yoked to Jesus! And when we take His yoke upon us, we will find it is easy, and we will rest! (Matt. 11:29-30). Glory to God!

> *"And I testify again to every man who becomes circumcised that he is a debtor to keep the whole law"* (Gal. 5:3).

The only man that has ever kept the whole law was Jesus! If we are guilty of one point of the law, we are guilty of the whole law (James 2:10).

How do we make a law out of a good thing like fasting? By moving our faith off the cross exclusively and looking to fasting for victory in our lives. "Look at me, Lord, I fasted, I'm more holy now! That sin that was bothering me is gone!" No! You may have a temporary reprieve from that particular sin, but fasting does not deliver us from sin. Only our faith in the blood of Jesus gives us victory over sin! If our faith is in our fasting for victory, then we are trying to progressively sanctify ourselves. We are attempting to make ourselves holy and set ourselves apart by fasting.

The sanctification process is not by what we do. It is by faith in what Jesus did on the cross. The Christian discipline of fasting to seek God's face for direction in our lives is biblical. However, when we put our faith in fasting to defeat sin, or to please God, we have just turned fasting into a law.

There is a twenty-one-day fasting program in Christian bookstores as I write this. It is a law that will strengthen the sin nature and put people in bondage (I Cor. 15:56). When the Christian looks to Christian disciplines as the way of victory, they are only setting themselves up for failure. For example, on day fifteen of this twenty-one-day fast, they ate. Now, they feel like they failed God because they broke the law.

The reader may be saying, "Well, you're taking this too far." No, not when it comes to how to live for God. This should be the believer's number one goal in life. If this system of fasting for victory in the Christian's life were biblical, then everybody would be able to do it.

My mother loved God. She was seventy-six years old and weighed one hundred pounds. Do you think she could survive a twenty-one-day fast? God is not going to give us something for victory in our lives that not all believers can do. But each and every believer can grow in the grace and the knowledge of Him by keeping their faith in Jesus Christ and Him crucified! Fasting is biblical, and we should all fast for direction in our lives, but not to make ourselves holy before God or to defeat sin. Our faith must be in Christ Jesus and must always include His finished work of the cross! Thank You, Jesus, for the simplicity of the gospel.

> "You have become estranged from Christ, you who attempt to be justified by law; you have fallen from grace" (Gal. 5:4).

Falling from grace is not sinning! Falling from grace is going back to law! Let the reader see this great truth. When the Christian sins, he does not fall from grace if his faith is still in Christ. He is still under grace! But when we go back and add law to the grace that saved us, we are frustrating or hindering, the grace of God (Gal. 2:21). We are trying to obtain righteousness by a law.

The first time the Holy Spirit revealed this truth to me it strengthened my walk with the Lord in a very big way. Read this verse again. When we try to justify ourselves by law, we will become estranged from Christ, and the cross will become of none effect to us. Even good Christian disciplines like prayer, Bible reading, and going to church can become laws if we put our faith in them.

When we move our faith off the cross, we fall from grace! Grace is something we must grow in daily. No one has arrived at the point where they can say, "I've got this!" No, we must *continuously* fight the good fight of faith. Even the apostle Paul, whom God used to write the verses we are studying said, *"Brethren, I do not count myself to have apprehended; but one thing I do, forgetting those things which are behind and reaching forward to those things which are ahead, I press toward the goal for the prize of the upward call of God in Christ Jesus"* (Phil. 3:13-14).

As we continue to learn how to live for God, we must look at the all-important difference between walking in the Spirit and walking in the flesh.

> *"For the flesh lusts against the Spirit, and the Spirit against the flesh; and these are contrary to one another, so that you do not do the things that you wish"* (Gal. 5:17).

The Bible tells us that our flesh is fighting against the Spirit. Someone might say, "My flesh is not fighting the Holy Spirit!" The Word of God does not change or ever lie. Therefore, we need to understand what the Holy Spirit is saying here. There is a big difference between justification and progressive sanctification!

Before we are saved, the Holy Spirit is outside of us and fighting for us. The Holy Spirit is convicting us of our sin and drawing us to acceptance of Jesus Christ's sacrifice on the cross that paid for our sin. The Holy Spirit is outside speaking to us with that still, small voice, "You are a sinner. You need a Savior. You broke the laws of God. Give your life to Jesus. He died on the cross for you," God uses the law lawfully to convict us of our sin.

However, once we are saved and justified, the Holy Spirit then comes and lives on the inside of us. Immediately, the battle between the Spirit and the flesh begins! The Holy Spirit is now on the inside of us and fighting against our flesh. Now the Holy Spirit whispers with a still, small voice, "You're a Christian now. We don't talk like that. We don't dress like that. Read your Bible, go to church." The Holy Spirit is saying, "Keep your faith in the cross of Jesus. Jesus will sanctify you; the blood of Jesus is your answer for everything."

We have now entered into the progressive sanctification process. God is not using law anymore. The Holy Spirit is operating differently now than how He did before we were saved and under law. The Holy Spirit is now fighting inside of us and against our flesh.

Our flesh likes law! When we are under law, we try to sanctify ourselves, which is not possible. We try to help God, but we end up fighting against the Holy Spirit. According to this verse, when we do this, you will not do the things that you will. The Christian living under law will fulfill the lust of the flesh and produce works of the flesh. But if we back up to verse 16, we will see the way out of this dilemma.

> *"I say then: Walk in the Spirit, and you shall not fulfill the lust of the flesh"* (Gal. 5:16).

In the Greek, the word *lust* is *epithymia*. It is singular (the lust of the flesh) not plural (lusts of the flesh). What is the lust of the flesh? It is going back to law! Our flesh loves law, desires law. Any law! Again, anything and everything we put our faith in other than the cross of Christ becomes a law to us.

In our attempt to keep the law, we deceitfully think we have a part in our sanctification process. I hear the standard argument, "Are you saying that we don't have to do anything?" Please don't insult yourself! Of course we have to do something. We have to keep our faith in the finished work of Jesus!

That is not as easy as it sounds because our flesh is lusting against the Spirit. But if we walk in the Spirit, we will not fulfill the lust of the flesh. Notice that the Word of God does not say the lust of the flesh will not be there. It will be there until we are glorified. If we walk in the Spirit, we will not fulfill the lust of the flesh, which is going back to law in trying to please God.

How do we walk in the Spirit? The Holy Spirit in me, the same Holy Spirit that is in you, will always, always point us to Jesus Christ and His finished work of the cross! He will not point to a program or system of man. He will not glorify a man! The Holy Spirit, who lives inside of us and is fighting with our stinking flesh, will always lead us to put our faith in Jesus Christ and Him crucified! The blood! The cross!

When our faith is exclusively in Jesus Christ and His finished work of the cross, we are walking in the Spirit! That is where the victory was won. That is the grace of God! For by

CHAPTER TWENTY HOW TO WALK IN THE SPIRIT | 187

grace you have been saved (the cross) through faith. We walk in the Spirit by keeping our faith in the sacrifice of God's Son. Jesus said when the Spirit comes, *"He will glorify Me"* (John 16:14). *"And this is the victory that has overcome the world—our faith"* (I John 5:4). The Holy Spirit will have us walking in the faith of the Son of God.

> *"But if you are led by the Spirit, you are not under law"* (Gal. 5:18).

This verse should nail shut any doubt of what the lust of the flesh is. It is the returning to law. *"If you are led by the Spirit, you are not under law."* Faith in anything other than Jesus Christ and Him crucified is a law. If we look to a man-made program, we are then walking in the flesh.

It is the job of the Holy Spirit to conform us into the image of Christ. With our faith in the cross, the Holy Spirit then has the liberty to move on our behalf. It is then that we will grow in the grace and knowledge of Jesus Christ (II Peter 3:18). This is the only way to grow in grace! We must not fall from grace and go back to law!

> *"Now the works of the flesh are evident, which are: adultery, fornication, uncleanness, lewdness, idolatry, sorcery, hatred, contentions, jealousies, outbursts of wrath, selfish ambitions, dissensions, heresies, envy, murders, drunkenness, revelries, and the like; of which I tell you beforehand,*

> *just as I also told you in time past, that those who practice such things will not inherit the kingdom of God"* (Gal. 5:19-21).

The Word of God tells us what the works of the flesh are. The works of the flesh are the result of the lust of the flesh. These are two different things. The lust of the flesh, which is going back to law, produces the works of the flesh. When we try to live for God by law, any law, we will fulfill the lust of the flesh and then the works of the flesh will manifest.

The law brought us to Christ but has no power to justify or sanctify us. The law is the strength of sin. If we are having a problem with the sin nature, it is because we have succumbed to the lust of the flesh and gone back to law, which is now producing the works of the flesh.

Faith in Christ alone gives the Holy Spirit the legal right to intervene in our lives. Now we are walking in the Spirit! The Holy Spirit will always point us to the cross of Christ where the victory was won. If we walk in the Spirit, we will not fulfill the lust of our stinking, rotten flesh! Glory to God and the Lamb forever!

This is not a license to sin, which the apostle Paul was accused of preaching. God forbid! In Galatians 5:21, the Holy Spirit is not saying that if we give in to the lust of the flesh (go back to law) that the works of the flesh will send us to hell. However, the Holy Spirit is saying that those who *"practice such things will not inherit the kingdom of God."*

CHAPTER TWENTY HOW TO WALK IN THE SPIRIT | 189

There is no license to sin! God is not going to send us to hell if we are selfish or for an outburst of wrath. If our faith remains in the blood of Jesus, even when we sin, *"we have an Advocate with the Father, Jesus Christ the righteous"* (I John 2:1). However, the Christian that is sinning without repentance will not make heaven his home; he is practicing sin! A scary thought, that once again refutes the unscriptural doctrine of once saved always saved.

> *"But the fruit of the Spirit is love, joy, peace, longsuffering, kindness, goodness, faithfulness, gentleness, self-control. Against such there is no law. And those who are Christ's have crucified the flesh with its passions and desires"* (Gal. 5:22-24).

Glory to God for the fruit of the Spirit! Fruit will grow in our lives as we walk in the Spirit by keeping our faith in the cross. Please notice that one of the fruits of the Spirit is self-control. We cannot even control ourselves without faith in Jesus! That is why Jesus said we must deny self to follow Him (Luke 9:23). You do not need a law against this wonderful fruit of the Spirit.

How do we crucify the flesh? By gritting our teeth and fighting the lust of the flesh? No, by simply walking in the Spirit! If you can get a hold of these great truths and believe what the Holy Spirit gave us through the apostle Paul, then you will see God's only way of victory—the cross!

How do we live for God in plain language:
By walking in the Spirit with our faith in the sacrifice of God's Son and only in the cross of Christ!

HOW TO LIVE FOR GOD

in plain language...

CHAPTER 21

THE LAW: WHEN, WHY, AND HOW?

CHAPTER TWENTY-ONE
THE LAW: WHEN, WHY, AND HOW?

I would like for us to examine the when, why, and how of the giving of the Ten Commandments and the ceremonial law.

Jesus fulfilled the law for us. Therefore, the Christian is to live under grace, not law. Although the law played a big part in bringing us to salvation, it is to have no part in us today. When we understand this, then true liberty can occur.

Looking at the timing of when God gave the law will help us better understand how the Christian is to handle the law given by God on Mount Sinai.

WHEN?

Sin entered the world through man in the garden of Eden when Adam rebelled against God (Rom. 5:12). It would seem to have been the perfect time for when God would have given the law. There were only two people on the earth, but God did not give the Ten Commandments to Adam and Eve. Instead, the grace of God provided a sacrifice.

> *"Also for Adam and his wife the Lord God made tunics of skin, and clothed them"* (Gen. 3:21).

God would have to shed the blood of an innocent animal to cover the guilty. This would point to the sacrifice of the Lamb of God that would one day take away the sin of the world. No law was given. The grace of God was there for Adam.

Hundreds of years after Adam, the wickedness of man was so great in the earth that the Lord was sorry, grieved in His heart, that He had made man (Gen. 6:5-6). Therefore, God said He would destroy man by a flood.

> *"But Noah found grace in the eyes of the Lord"* (Gen. 6:8).

Noah's name means rest. Rest found grace in the eyes of the Lord. Until the believer learns to rest in the finished work of Jesus, he will not grow in grace.

God had instructed Noah to build an ark, a type of Christ. When the flood came, all life was destroyed because of sin. Only Noah and his family were saved. They were inside the ark, just as we are in Christ.

Approximately fourteen months later, Noah and his family left the ark. They were the only eight people on the

CHAPTER TWENTY-ONE THE LAW: WHEN, WHY, AND HOW? | 195

earth. Would this be when God would give the law, the Ten Commandments, to live by? After all, God was, in effect, starting over with just Noah and his family. God could have said, "Noah, this is how you will live for Me, here are My commandments." But this is not when God would give the law!

Noah built an altar and sacrificed the clean animals, pointing to the cross of Christ (Gen. 8:20). With Noah's faith in what the animal sacrifice represented, God was pleased. Still, no law was given. The grace of God was there for Noah.

Four hundred years after the flood, God would establish His chosen people through Abraham. He called Abraham out from an idol worshipping family to a land He would later show him. God told Abraham that He was going to make him a great nation and the Messiah would come from his loins. This would seem like the perfect time for when God would give the Ten Commandments. But God did not give the Ten Commandments to Abraham when He established His new people. Why not?

God is a God of laws, but He never wanted His greatest creation, you and me, to live for Him by keeping the Ten Commandments. Not before Christ came and not now. The believer is to be governed by the spiritual laws and covenants that God has established and has never changed. God simply wants us to believe in Him!

God established His covenant by telling Abraham how He would handle the sin problem. This took place 430 years before he gave the Ten Commandments. God wants us to live by grace through faith!

> *"And the Scripture, foreseeing that God would justify the Gentiles by faith, preached the gospel to Abraham beforehand, saying, "In you all the nations shall be blessed"* (Gal. 3:8).

And Abraham believed God, and it was accounted to him for righteousness (Gen. 15:6). What is the gospel that Abraham believed? What is the good news? Jesus Christ and Him crucified!

The Abrahamic covenant was for the children of old to be righteous (Gen. 15:6).

The law of faith is for believers today to be justified (Rom. 3:26-28).

The law of the Spirit of life in Christ Jesus is for believers today to be sanctified (Rom. 8:2).

My prayer is that you see the heartbeat of God. The Lord our God does not want His people, you and me, to live under law. He did not give the Ten Commandments to Adam or Noah or Abraham. He gave the law to Moses at Mount Sinai, many hundreds of years after the creation.

The answer to when God gave the law is step one in understanding God's intentions regarding the Ten Commandments. From the time of creation to now, the grace of God was there.

The Holy Spirit, through Paul, will now answer the very important question of why. Why did God give His people the Ten Commandments?

WHY?

"What purpose then does the law serve? It was added because of transgressions, till the Seed should come to whom the promise was made" (Gal. 3:19).

Paul asks the churches of Galatia a rhetorical question, "What purpose does the law serve?" Or why did God give the law? God knew that even this very day we might be asking the question why. As always, the Word of God, authored by the Holy Spirit, answers the question for us. I would like to break this verse down word by word for clarity.

In the Greek, the word *added* is *prostithemi*. It has two different meanings, depending on the context in which it is used. The first meaning is "to be added to" something. For example, in Matthew 6:33, if we seek first the kingdom of God, then all these things shall be added to you. The Ten Commandments were not added to the Abrahamic covenant. If that were so, then God would have needed to change the covenant of promise, which He did not (Gal. 3:17).

In Galatians 3:19, the second meaning is "to be added alongside" of something. The law was added alongside the covenant God had made with Abraham. Abraham would be righteous by faith in the promised Messiah alone, not by keeping a law. The Abrahamic covenant was given to Abraham 430 years prior to God adding the Ten Commandments. The Ten Commandments are not part of the Abrahamic covenant! The Ten Commandments were not added to the covenant. They were added *alongside* the Abrahamic covenant and do not change the covenant.

In the Greek, *because* is *charin,* meaning "on account of, for the sake of, to show, or the reason it was given will follow." Also, in the Greek, *transgressions* is *parabasis,* meaning "wrongdoing, disregarding, violating." It is derived from the base word *parabaino,* meaning "contrary to, to violate, to go past or pass over without touching a thing, to neglect, to turn aside from, to depart or one who abandons his trust."

The law was added alongside of the Abrahamic covenant because the children of Israel had transgressed, violated, and gone past, God's covenant of righteousness by faith. They had neglected and turned aside from the covenant that God made with Abraham. That is the *why*! God gave the Ten Commandments to show the people they had violated the Abrahamic covenant.

Sin and transgression are two different things!

The Greek word for *sin* is *hamartano,* a verb meaning "to miss the mark, to fall short." Transgression is "a revolt or rebellion, coming out from under and going a different way." Brother Swaggart has defined transgression as "a breach of covenant." Transgression is a sin, but all sin is not transgression.

CHAPTER TWENTY-ONE THE LAW: WHEN, WHY, AND HOW? | 199

Let us look at an example. When I have an evil thought against my brother, I have sinned. I have fallen short, but I have not transgressed the covenant. My faith is still in Jesus Christ and Him crucified! Thank God, I am still in covenant by faith in the finished work of Christ.

The children of Israel were walking in the wilderness in unbelief. They were transgressing the Abrahamic covenant. Therefore, the law was added on Mount Sinai because the people were not keeping covenant with God by believing Him.

Sin and transgression are two different things:

- *"But Joshua said to the people, 'You cannot serve the Lord, for He is a holy God. He is a jealous God; He will not forgive your transgressions nor your sins'"* (Josh. 24:19).
- *"Do not remember the sins of my youth, nor my transgressions"* (Ps. 25:07).
- *"For I acknowledge my transgressions, and my sin is always before me"* (Ps. 51:3).
- *"I, even I, am He who blots out your transgressions for My own sake, And I will not remember your sins"* (Isa. 43:25).
- *"I have blotted out, like a thick cloud, your transgressions, and like a cloud, your sins"* (Isa. 44:22).

To *come out from under* the covenant, like the children of Israel did, is unbelief. This is far, far worse than a onetime act of sin. This is why the Lord gave the Ten Commandments, because of transgressions! It would show man that he was outside of the covenant and in need of a Savior. We are all born outside of the covenant, and that is why Jesus said, *"unless a man be born again, he cannot see the kingdom of God"* (John 3:3).

In the wilderness they did not believe that God would sustain them even though He had delivered them from Egyptian bondage. They were not offering sacrifices but were complaining to God and wanting to go back to Egypt. In their unbelief, they had carried idols with them out of Egypt. They were transgressing the Abrahamic covenant! Therefore, God gave them the law at Mount Sinai to show them they were sinning against Him and needed a Redeemer!

The word *until* in the Greek is *achri*, meaning a very specific period of time. How long would they, and you and I, remain under the Ten Commandments? Until the Seed would come! How long? Until the Seed, Jesus, comes (Gal. 3:16).

We were all born sinners, born under the Ten Commandments. We are not born in covenant with God. When we are born again and receive Jesus as our Lord and Savior, we then enter into the everlasting covenant! Jesus has come into our hearts and lives, and now we are no longer under the Ten Commandments!

> *"For Christ is the end of the law for righteousness to everyone who believes"* (Rom. 10:4).

Adam was a transgressor: *"Nevertheless death reigned from Adam to Moses, even over those who had not sinned according to the likeness of the transgression of Adam, who is a type of Him to come"* (Rom. 5:14).

Eve was a transgressor: *"And Adam was not deceived, but the woman being deceived, fell into transgression"* (I Tim. 2:14).

Judas was a transgressor: *"To take part in this ministry and apostleship from which Judas by transgression fell, that he might go to his own place"* (Acts 1:25).

David was a transgressor (but repented): *"Have mercy upon me, O God, According to Your lovingkindness; According to the multitude of Your tender mercies, Blot out my transgressions"* (Psalm 51:1).

The Ten Commandments remain today to show the unredeemed man that he is a sinner and a transgressor of the covenant of God. To show him that he is in need of a Savior!

We have seen the *when* and the *why*. Now we will look at the *how*. Prayerfully, through the Word of God, we will see how God felt as He gave His prized creation the Ten Commandments.

HOW?

I want you to feel the heartbeat of God the day He gave the Ten Commandments. His grace was there from the beginning and should have been sufficient. God did not want to give us laws to keep in order for us to come into covenant with Him.

He just wanted us to believe Him. He had already made a way for us to approach Him by the shedding of innocent blood, pointing to the cross of Jesus. Even with our own children, we want them to love us unconditionally, not because they keep a law we have given them. We just want them to trust and believe us. God wanted His people to simply believe that the promised Messiah would come.

How did God give the law? Up on a mountain. But oh, what a mountain it was that day!

> *"Then it came to pass on the third day, in the morning, that there were thunderings and lightnings, and a thick cloud on the mountain; and the sound of the trumpet was very loud, so that all the people who were in the camp trembled. And Moses brought the people out of the camp to meet with God, and they stood at the foot of the mountain. Now Mount Sinai was completely in smoke, because the Lord descended upon it in fire. Its smoke ascended like the smoke of a furnace, and the whole mountain quaked greatly. And when the blast of the trumpet sounded long and became louder and louder, Moses spoke, and God answered him by voice"* (Ex. 19:16-19).

How did God give the Ten Commandments after hundreds of years of His people living totally under grace? With thunderings, lightnings, and a thick cloud on a mountain with the sound of a very loud trumpet with all the people trembling.

The mountain was completely covered in smoke because the Lord descended on it in fire, and the whole mountain quaked greatly. Then the blast of the trumpet sounded long and became louder and louder!

That is how God gave the law! Can the reader feel it? What a moment in the history of man! God gave the law so we would see our need and come to Him and not be lost forever! And then, just before our loving, gracious, heavenly Father gave the law to His people, He reminds them, *"I am the Lord your God, who brought you out of the land of Egypt, out of the house of bondage"* (Ex. 20:2).

God is saying, "I brought you out of bondage, out of the land of Egypt!" We must understand that the Ten Commandments have a very specific purpose. They were given by God to show man that his sin had separated him from God, that he is a transgressor, out of the covenant, and in need of a Savior!

When we come to Jesus, we enter into the everlasting covenant and are no longer transgressors of the covenant! Glory to God! The Ten Commandments have done their job. Jesus has fulfilled the law for us. We are to live under grace and be governed by His spiritual laws, not the Ten Commandments. We must not mix law with God's grace.

The law was there for a very specific period of time, until the Seed would come! We are no longer under the Ten Commandments. God never intended for the Ten Commandments to sanctify us! So why do we try to keep the Ten Commandments, or the law, in a foolish effort to sanctify ourselves?

Thank God we are no longer transgressors; we are now in the covenant! When the believer goes back to law of any kind, to defeat sin or please God, he is saying that what Jesus did on the cross was not enough! And when we find ourselves in that position, we must repent and return to faith in Christ alone!

> *"Is the law then against the promises of God? Certainly not! For if there had been a law given which could have given life, truly righteousness would have been by the law. But the Scripture has confined all under sin, that the promise by faith in Jesus Christ might be given to those who believe"* (Gal. 3:21-22).

The law shows us the character of God. God is holy and righteous. The law is holy and right. The law is from God, but the law was never intended to make us holy and righteous. If God could have made a law that we could keep that could redeem us, then He would not have had to send His Son to die a cruel death on the cross! But thank God for Jesus and His finished work of the cross.

We were not justified by obeying a law. We were justified when we entered into the everlasting covenant through faith in the sacrifice of God's Son (Rom. 3:20-21). We are not being sanctified by obeying a law. We are being sanctified through faith in the offering of the body of Jesus Christ (Heb. 10:14).

The cross! The cross! The cross! We receive the promise of righteousness by faith in Christ Jesus and Him crucified.

CHAPTER TWENTY-ONE THE LAW: WHEN, WHY, AND HOW?

Jesus is the promised one. Jesus cut the covenant between God and man on the cross! It is a blood covenant. Jesus is the new covenant!

> *"But before faith came, we were kept under guard by the law, kept for the faith which would afterward be revealed"* (Galatians 3:23).

The word *kept* means "to be locked up." We were locked up and kept under guard with no escape from the law. But after faith was revealed, we were set free from the law! Do we truly understand what the Lord is writing here in His Word? Until we can answer and understand the three questions of when, why, and how the Ten Commandments were given, we will not be totally free from law.

The commandments had a very important purpose, but that *purpose was* realized when we said yes to God's redemption plan and entered into the everlasting covenant! Hallelujah!

> *"Therefore the law was our tutor to bring us to Christ, that we might be justified by faith"* (Gal. 3:24).

The law was given on Mount Sinai many hundreds of years after creation to teach us that the sin of unbelief makes us a transgressor of the covenant. The law would show us that, due to our sin, we were not in relationship with our Creator.

The law would also teach us that we must be justified by faith alone in the sacrifice of God's Son on the cross.

> *"But after faith has come, we are no longer under a tutor"* (Gal. 3:25).

Glory to God! We are no longer under law! Salvation has come to you and me by faith alone. The law has done its job and has taught us well. We are no longer transgressors, but our sins are now washed by the blood, and we are in covenant with our holy God! The law, of course, is still there for the unbeliever. However, we, as Christians, are dead to the law (Rom. 7:4). Our relationship with the law ended when we accepted Jesus as the sacrifice for our sin!

We need to know this!

> *"Knowing this: that the law is not for the righteous person, but for the lawless and insubordinate"* (I Tim. 1:9).

Brothers and sisters in Christ, we are righteous by faith alone! God has set us free from His own Ten Commandments! So why do we follow the laws of a man or denomination? If God Himself could not justify us by a law, but had to send His only Son to die, then why do we think we can live for God by laws?

We make laws because we think we can then do something to make ourselves holy. All our heavenly Father wants us to do to please Him is to believe in Him (Heb. 11:6). Paul had to repent of looking to law. The foolish Galatians had to repent of taking their eyes off of Christ crucified. I had to repent of faith in my prayer meetings to please God. Is there a law you have made in order to please God? Anything that is not faith in the cross of Jesus becomes a law to you!

How to live for God in plain language:
Under grace, not law! Repent of faith in anything besides Jesus Christ and Him crucified and begin living the abundant life Jesus promised!

HOW TO LIVE FOR GOD
in plain language...

CHAPTER 22

SANCTIFYING REST

CHAPTER TWENTY-TWO
SANCTIFYING REST

In Hebrews 4, we are told of the promise of entering into His rest. It is not the rest that a poor, pathetic man can give, but the rest that only God can give, the sanctifying rest!

> "Therefore, since a promise remains of entering His rest, let us fear lest any of you seem to have come short of it. For indeed the gospel was preached to us as well as to them; but the word which they heard did not profit them, not being mixed with faith in those who heard it. For we who have believed do enter that rest, as He has said: 'So I swore in My wrath, "They shall not enter My rest,"' although the works were finished from the foundation of the world" (Heb. 4:1-3).

The Word of God tells us that the same rest that the children of Israel did not enter into because of their unbelief, is the same rest available to believers today. It is God's desire that we enter into His rest, but it is not automatic. Some Christians think, "Now that I'm saved, I will just wait for the rapture," or, "Now that I am baptized in the Holy Spirit, I have arrived." These Scriptures tell the believer that we should fear lest any of us seem to come short of entering into God's rest.

God swore in His wrath that all of those who came out of Egypt would not enter the sanctifying rest because of their unbelief (Heb. 3:16). They would die in the wilderness without crossing the Jordan. It would be their unbelief that would keep them from entering into His sanctifying rest.

The Greek word for *rest*, found in Hebrews 4:1 and 3 is *katapausis*. It means "to cease from labor, the act of resting, a place of rest, a dwelling or abode." It is a noun. It is the sanctifying rest that we have by faith in Christ. It is a place that God has provided for us to live, to dwell.

The promised land in the Old Testament was to represent the rest that God gives His children that trust in Him and Him alone. It did not symbolize heaven. Moses did not cross the Jordan River into the promised land, but Moses is in heaven today. When God's children finally crossed the Jordan River, into the promised land, there were Amorites, Jebusites, and Hivites—all enemies to be defeated. That is not how it is or will be in heaven. However, for the Christian in this life, we will face many enemies that God will defeat as we rest in Him. The promised land is a place that God has provided for all that believe Him. It is a place that, when we enter, even in the face of the enemy, we can rest!

As we study God's people and their journey through the wilderness, we will see through typology how God showed His people the sanctification process. The sanctification process is no different today than it was thousands of years ago. It is by faith! But that faith must have the proper object. That is why He said in Hebrews 4:1 that we should fear lest any of us seem to come short of entering His rest. He is not talking about the eternal rest in heaven, but the peaceful, sanctifying rest He provided on this earth as we walk by faith.

We begin with the children of God being enslaved to Pharaoh for 400 years, just as we were slaves to the devil before Jesus saved us. Pharaoh, a type of the devil, would not let God's people go easily. Satan is a hard taskmaster, and there is no freedom. But one day, glory to God, the Lord told Moses to go tell Pharaoh, "Let My people go!" (Ex. 5:1). But when did Pharaoh let God's people go? Miracle after miracle of flies, locusts, and frogs all over the land, and still Pharaoh would not let God's people go. God still does miracles today. I believe in miracles, but miracles do not set us free from the powers of darkness or sin. Only the blood of Jesus can deliver us!

God told Moses: *"Speak to all the congregation of Israel, saying: 'On the tenth of this month every man shall take for himself a lamb, according to the house of his father, a lamb for a household"* (Ex. 12:3).

> *"And they shall take some of the blood and put it on the two doorposts and on the lintel of the houses where they eat it"* (Ex. 12:7).

Why the blood of an innocent lamb? *"Without shedding of blood there is no remission [of sin]"* (Heb. 9:22). Everything we read in the Old Testament points to the sacrifice of God's Son. I want you to hear and see from the Scriptures that the Bible is the account of the fall of man and the redemption of man through the blood of Jesus shed on the cross. The redeemed man can then, and only then, enter the sanctifying rest that the Lord has for him.

> *"Now the blood shall be a sign for you on the houses where you are. And when I see the blood, I will pass over you; and the plague shall not be on you to destroy you when I strike the land of Egypt"* (Ex. 12:13).

God said, "When I see the blood, I will pass over you!" The children of Israel were safe and secure under the blood that night when the death angel came, and all the firstborn in Egypt would die. The next day, God's people walked out of bondage and were set free after 400 years of slavery! God now applies the shed blood of the Lamb to our lives, and we are delivered out of slavery! The blood pointed to what Jesus, the Lamb of God, would do on the cross by giving His life for ours.

CHAPTER TWENTY-TWO SANCTIFYING REST | 215

Now God will lead His children into the wilderness. You and I, like them, are in a wilderness, but God led us here. After just a few days, they come to the Red Sea and are unable to cross. They look back and see Pharaoh and all of his army coming after them. The devil is not going to just let us go after we are saved by the blood of the Lamb. We have changed sides in this spiritual war, and he wants us back. The Red Sea is a big problem. They cannot swim the Red Sea just as we cannot defeat many problems in our lives. This is where we need to learn to rest.

> *"And Moses said to the people, "Do not be afraid. Stand still, and see the salvation of the Lord, which He will accomplish for you today. For the Egyptians whom you see today, you shall see again no more forever. The Lord will fight for you, and you shall hold your peace"* (Ex. 14:13-14).

The children of God wanted to go back to Egypt—Egypt being a type of the world. The world has nothing but slavery, sin, heartache, death, and destruction! Moses then said, "Do not be afraid, stand still, and see the salvation of the Lord." Here they will get their first lesson in the progressive sanctification process, and so will we.

When a Christian has a problem in their life like the Red Sea, we need to stand still! If we do not stand still and let God handle our problems, then we will not see the salvation of the Lord. But when we stop and rest in Christ, we will see Him meet our every need. The problem will still be there for a time of testing, but we will not see the situation. We will see the salvation of the Lord! Glory to God!

What is your problem today, Christian? Are you saved by the blood but wandering in the wilderness with a big problem? Do not fight the situation, fight the good fight of faith! When we rest with our faith in the crucified Christ, we will not only be delivered, but we will not see the enemy anymore. Our focus will not be on the problem or the devil, but on the victory that Jesus won for us on the cross!

So how did God take care of this enormous problem?

> *"But lift up your rod, and stretch out your hand over the sea and divide it. And the children of Israel shall go on dry ground through the midst of the sea"* (Ex. 14:16).

God told Moses to lift up his rod, a wooden rod—a type of the cross—to hold it up over the Red Sea. Not the blue sea or the green sea but the Red Sea, a type of the blood of Jesus. Then in Exodus 14:21, we read that as Moses held the rod over the Red Sea, a strong east wind—a type of the Holy Spirit—came and made the sea into dry land.

As the believer looks exclusively to the blood of Jesus, he will cease from his own works and rest in Christ. The children of Israel walked across on dry ground, and when they looked back, they did not see Pharaoh. He was drowned in the Red Sea! Glory to God! The devil was defeated in the Red Sea by the blood!

We must stand still and rest, looking to the cross where Jesus shed His blood. Then, the Holy Spirit will move in our lives. This is God's means of progressive sanctification. The only way the Holy Spirit can help us in a time of need is for us to rest in the finished work of the cross. The Holy Spirit will not help us if we are looking to a program of man. He works exclusively as we rest in what Jesus did on the cross.

> *"So Moses brought Israel from the Red Sea; then they went out into the Wilderness of Shur. And they went three days in the wilderness and found no water. Now when they came to Marah, they could not drink the waters of Marah, for they were bitter, Therefore the name of it was called Marah. And the people complained against Moses, saying, 'What shall we drink?'"* (Ex. 15:22-24).

Just three short days after walking across the Red Sea on dry ground and seeing Pharaoh's army drowned in the Red Sea, they found themselves with nothing but bitter water. I am sure we all could look back on them today and say, "Hey, children of God, what were you worried about? God delivered you by the blood on the doorpost, and He defeated Pharaoh at the Red Sea. Just believe Him now for water!"

Are we not guilty of the same thing, of not letting God progressively sanctify us by faith in the blood alone? Are we resting in the finished work of the cross? Do we Christians who are saved by the blood think we will have the sanctifying rest by going to church, or reading so many chapters of the Bible a day? Or think if we fast and go to all the prayer meetings that we will be more sanctified?

These are all good Christian disciplines that we should do, but they do not make us holy and righteous! They do not deliver and continuously sanctify the believer. Faith in our Christian disciplines will not bring rest for our souls. It is your faith in the blood and only faith in the blood that will give you that rest and sanctify you!

God has provided a rest for you to enter into by faith just as he did for the children of Israel in the wilderness. However, they complained and would not enter into His rest. We are talking about God's people! The ones He delivered by the blood!

The Holy Spirit is talking to you right now. You cannot set yourself apart or make yourself holy by some man-made system. Our faith must be exclusively in the cross of Christ, or we may bring the wrath of God upon us and not have that sanctifying rest He promised (Heb. 4:3).

> *"So he cried out to the Lord, and the Lord showed him a tree. When he cast it into the waters, the waters were made sweet. There He made a statute and an ordinance for them, and there He tested them"* (Ex. 15:25).

Sometimes in our Christian walk life can be bitter. Maybe someone did us wrong years ago, and we are still bitter toward that person, or even God. We want to drink this water of life, but it is bitter.

God showed Moses a tree, a type of the cross. When he put the tree in the waters, the waters were made sweet. When we look to the cross, our bitterness will be made sweet! Thank You, Jesus!

The cross is not just for salvation! It is for every need of the believer. Nowhere in the Bible do we read about them removing the tree. We are to come back to our faith in the cross alone for everyday life, and it will be sweet again.

We now see, as they continue in the wilderness where God led them, they become hungry. Are you hungry for more of God?

> *"Then the whole congregation of the children of Israel complained against Moses and Aaron in the wilderness. And the children of Israel said to them, 'Oh, that we had died by the hand of the Lord in the land of Egypt, when we sat by the pots of meat and when we ate bread to the full! For you have brought us out into this wilderness to kill this whole assembly with hunger'"* (Ex. 16:2-3).

Two months after leaving Egypt, the children of God that were delivered by the blood, crossed the Red Sea, and saw the bitter waters made sweet were now hungry. They are complaining against God who had already performed amazing miracles that they had seen with their own eyes. Once again, they are in unbelief, wanting to go back to slavery, back to Egypt, which is a type of the world. They refused to rest and trust in the Lord.

Do you really think that as slaves of Pharaoh they ate pots of meat to the full? The devil is a liar and the father of lies. The world has nothing for the child of God. God wants us to rest by faith in the finished work of the cross so we will not hunger.

The Lord only has good for us. He wants to teach us to *depend* on Him and Him alone. Not dependency on ourselves, or a man, or a system of man, or the newest fad in the bookstores. No! We have one book, the Bible! And one way! Jesus said, *"I am the way"* (John 14:6). Does that mean that all books are bad? Heavens no, you're reading this book! However, the book must be centered on the crucified Christ, or it is of no value to the believer and will actually do them harm.

Let the Holy Spirit reveal to you through the wilderness experience the progressive sanctification process. Let Him show you how to live for God!

> *"Then the Lord said to Moses, 'Behold, I will rain bread from heaven for you. And the people shall go out and gather a certain quota every day, that I may test them, whether they will walk in My law or not"* (Ex. 16:4).

They had to gather the manna every day. His body was broken on the cross, and we must look to the cross every day! It is a life-and-death situation! The children of Israel were already saved by the blood, just like us. But once again, the Lord points them, and us, to the body of Christ—the cross—when we are dying of hunger. The bread is a type of Christ's broken body on the cross. Jesus said, *"I am the bread of life"* (John 6:48). The bread comes from heaven. Not from the ground, not from a man, but from heaven. Please hear that loud and clear! Nothing else will satisfy our spiritual hunger except the cross of Christ! If we do not eat the Bread of Life, we will die.

God said, *"That I may test them."* Hello, Christian, we are in a test! What is the test? Whether we will walk in His law or not. But wait! The Ten Commandments had not been given yet. So the law is whether they would believe Him and go gather the manna every day. Will we look to the finished work of the cross for our sanctification process every day, or will we move our faith to something else when we are hungry for more of God? Are you a hungry Christian? Hungry for more of God? This is how God tests our faith, to see if we believe that His provision is sufficient.

> *"Therefore the people contended with Moses, and said, 'Give us water, that we may drink.' So Moses said to them, 'Why do you contend with me? Why do you tempt the Lord?'"* (Ex. 17:2).

Once again, the children of God are thirsty and complaining. They are not resting in what the Lord had provided, the blood sacrifice, pointing to the Messiah to come. In their hearts, they want to go back to Egypt, a type of the world. I see this today as I travel the world. Christians are trying everything that carnal man throws at them. Where is the discernment? Why do we think we can sanctify ourselves and find rest for our souls in the systems and programs of man? One more time, God, through the wilderness experience, will show them and us how to live for God.

> *"And the Lord said to Moses, 'Go on before the people, and take with you some of the elders of Israel. Also take in your hand your rod with which you struck the river, and go. Behold, I will stand before you there on the rock in Horeb; and you shall strike the rock, and water will come out of it, that the people may drink.' And Moses did so in the sight of the elders of Israel"* (Exodus 17:5-6).

God told Moses, take your rod, your wooden rod—a type of the cross—and strike the rock. First Corinthians 10:4 says, *"that Rock was Christ."* When the Rock was struck, the water—a type of the Holy Spirit—flowed out to quench the thirst of every child of God. When we as believers are thirsty for more of God, we must look to the cross of Christ where He was crucified for our every need. Then and only then will the Holy Spirit move in our lives. This is the progressive sanctification process that we are to rest in until the day we are glorified. The entirety of the Bible points to the sacrifice of God's Son.

We have seen in these chapters of Exodus that God continuously tests His children to see if they will believe Him or not. He does not want us to live for Him by any other means than the faith in the sacrifice of His Son. Because of their unbelief, He swore in His wrath that they would not enter His rest. Let us fear, because we also will not enter that sanctifying rest without proper faith in the cross of Christ. The Holy Spirit only works in our lives as we look to the cross!

When we learn to rest in the finished work of Jesus, the Holy Spirit moves in our lives, and He sanctifies us!

> *"There remains therefore a rest for the people of God"* (Heb. 4:9).

In this verse, the Greek word *rest* is *sabbatismos,* which means "eternal rest, heaven." One day, if we keep our faith in the cross of Christ, we will see each other in heaven. But for now, we can enjoy the *katapausis*, sanctifying rest. How? Read on.

> *"For he who has entered His rest has himself also ceased from his own works as God did from His"* (Heb. 4:10).

The word *rest* here is, once again, *katapausis* in the Greek. It is His sanctifying rest that we have by simple faith in the finished work of Jesus on the cross. It is the refreshing rest we experience as we are laboring for the Lord. Therefore, we must cease from our own works in trying to sanctify ourselves. Let us look at God talking about His work, the creation, that He ceased from.

> *"And on the seventh day God ended His work which He had done, and He rested on the seventh day from all His work which He had done. Then God blessed the seventh day and sanctified it, because in it He rested from all His work which God had created and made"* (Gen. 2:2-3).

God rested on the seventh day from all His work, creation. God did not rest because He was tired! He rested because it was finished, and He sanctified it! It is the same for us today. We must look to the cross where Jesus said with a loud voice, "It is finished," and rest in His sanctification.

Pastor Sergi from Tanzania said, "I have learned from the message of the cross that when I work, God rests, but when I rest, God goes to work!" Just like at the Red Sea, God said, "Stand still and see the salvation of the Lord." If we do not rest—stand still in the finished work of the Lord, the cross—then we will not see when He works for us.

Now of course we labor, and of course we have to do something. Let us look at the next verse in Hebrews 4.

> *"Let us therefore be diligent* [labor] *to enter that rest, lest anyone fall according to the same example of disobedience"* (Heb. 4:11).

Our labor is to enter His sanctifying rest. God calls unbelief disobedience! We must be diligent to enter that place of rest. The children in the wilderness were disobedient and would not believe Him for their needs. So He swore in His wrath they would not enter His *katapausis*, sanctifying rest. He did not say they would not enter His *sabbatismos*, heaven.

Many Christians today are saved by the blood and on their way to heaven. However, they are struggling in their everyday life because of improperly placing their faith in something other than the cross for their daily sanctification. They are not enjoying the abundant life that Jesus promised. They are not resting in the finished work of the cross!

If you are reading this today and recognize that you are the same as the children of old, simply repent! Come back to your first love! Come back to faith in the blood of Jesus for every need in your life! Come back to the cross! In Acts 26:18, Jesus said we are *"sanctified by faith in Me."* We are continuously made holy and set apart by God Himself and not by our own willpower.

"As it is written, 'The just shall live by faith'" (Rom. 1:17)

But faith in what? Faith in the sacrifice of God's Son, and only the finished work of Jesus!

How to live for God in plain language:
Rest in the finished work of the cross!

HOW TO LIVE FOR GOD
in plain language...

CHAPTER 23

CRUCIFIED WITH CHRIST

CHAPTER TWENTY-THREE
CRUCIFIED WITH CHRIST

In Galatians 2:20, Paul makes the all-important proclamation, *"I have been crucified with Christ."* To understand this statement, we must first begin with Chapter 1 verse 6 of his letter to the church of Galatia.

> *"I marvel that you are turning away so soon from Him who called you in the grace of Christ, to a different gospel"* (Gal. 1:6).

These are very strong words from the apostle, but let us understand that these words were by the Holy Spirit Himself. The "Him" in this verse is the Holy Spirit, the very one that the church of Galatia was turning away from. This turning away from the Holy Spirit is the same thing happening in most churches today. Why? How? Because most of the churches are looking to a law or church rules instead of the grace of God.

These laws and rules are a different gospel! We must not add to our faith! When we do this, either through a self-help program, psychology, or anything else, we are turning away from the Holy Spirit!

When we try to progressively sanctify ourselves, make ourselves acceptable to God, we are denying the finished work of the cross as being sufficient for all of our needs. If our faith is not exclusively in Jesus Christ and Him crucified for every need in our lives—salvation, healing, deliverance, sanctification, and the list goes on—then it is a different gospel! We are turning away from God.

I remember quite well the day that I realized I was trying to sanctify myself by my performance instead of by simple faith in the cross of my Jesus. It was shocking to discover that I had been turning away from the Holy Spirit! I would have never said it that way but, unfortunately, I had been looking to my own efforts to please God. My faith was still in the cross for salvation, but I had turned away from the leading and guiding of the Holy Spirit and was trying to sanctify myself by doing the Christian disciplines. Sadly, this brought condemnation and failures because I was looking to something other than the finished work of Jesus.

As a result, the Holy Spirit could not help me! Oh, I believed in the power of the cross theologically, but I was not living by faith in the cross. It was faith in Jesus and fourteen other things such as church attendance, prayer meetings, fasting, Bible reading and more in my attempt to please God and be holy. But when I began to understand the message of the cross and believe that the power was in the blood, then my failures turned into His victories (I Cor. 1:18). Glory to God! The Holy Spirit began to show me areas of my walk where I was not trusting God's provision, but rather trusting something else. I did a lot of repenting (rethinking) as the Lord began to reveal to me how to live for God. This revelation of the cross continues today.

You might be saying to yourself, "I am not turning away from God when I am using man's new plan on how to live for Him." The Holy Spirit through the apostle Paul says you are! The Holy Spirit will only point us to Jesus! He will not lift up a man or the system of man. He will only glorify Jesus! Why is it so hard for Christians to simply believe and live by faith alone in the cross of Christ? These man-made systems and programs are a different gospel! The gospel must not be altered. The Holy Spirit is telling each of us to not turn away to another gospel for any need in our lives.

> *"Which is not another; but there are some who trouble you and want to pervert the gospel of Christ. But even if we, or an angel from heaven, preach any other gospel to you than what we have preached to you, let him be accursed"* (Gal. 1:7-8).

Verse 7 states, *"there are some who ... want to pervert the gospel of Christ."* Man will always want to change us into the image of man. This perverts the gospel. Take a minute right now and think about the hundreds of programs in the Christian bookstore today. Most do not point the believer to Jesus because they are not Christ-centered. Most of the systems that man comes up with want us to follow man: "Do this or do that," or, "Do it like I tell you, and you will have a better Christian experience," or, "Be like me." The Holy Spirit, on the other hand, wants to conform us into the image of Christ. We must die to self, die to law, die to the sin nature, die to these efforts of man trying to control us! We must look only unto Jesus, the author and finisher of our faith.

In verse 8, the Holy Spirit continues by giving us a very stern warning of what happens when we turn away. If the message is not completely centered on the cross of Christ, it is a different gospel, and we will be accursed!

The remainder of Galatians 1 through Galatians 2:10 is a challenge by the apostle Paul for us to examine ourselves to see if our faith is in man or God. In Galatians 2:11-21, Paul will recount his journey to Jerusalem. This letter to the churches of Galatia will show that the apostle Paul was no respecter of persons. He had determined to know nothing among them, save Jesus Christ and Him crucified (I Cor. 2:2). Paul will have to go face-to-face with Peter and publicly rebuke him for putting the Gentiles back under law.

> "Now when Peter had come to Antioch, I withstood him to his face, because he was to be blamed" (Gal. 2:11).

CHAPTER TWENTY-THREE **CRUCIFIED WITH CHRIST** | **233**

Think about this encounter. It had to be very intense! Paul is not talking to an unbeliever! He is talking to the apostle Peter, the one who had walked with Jesus and was used after the ascension to preach the first message to the Jewish leaders. Peter, the man to whom God gave the vision of the animals coming down from heaven and said, *"kill and eat."* That vision showed Peter that the gospel was for all of mankind, not only the Jews (Acts 10:11-13). However, when Peter saw the Jews from Antioch coming, he would play the hypocrite by separating himself from the Gentiles.

> *"But when I saw that they were not straightforward about the truth of the gospel, I said to Peter before them all, 'If you, being a Jew, live in the manner of Gentiles and not as the Jews, why do you compel Gentiles to live as Jews? We who are Jews by nature, and not sinners of the Gentiles'"* (Gal. 2:14-15).

Notice the quotation marks the scholars used beginning in verse 14 to the end of the chapter [in NKJV]. These marks denote the actual words spoken by Paul to Peter. Paul is saying, "Peter, why are you putting these Gentiles under the Jewish law? We are born Jews, and God gave us the law, but even we cannot keep the law! So why are you trying to compel the Gentiles to live as Jews?"

The Apostle Paul here is protecting and defending the true gospel, as we must do also! If we believe that everything was finished on the cross, then we must not be carried away with the newest Christian fad, even if everyone seems to be doing it.

> *"Knowing that a man is not justified by the works of the law but by faith in Jesus Christ, even we have believed in Christ Jesus, that we might be justified by faith in Christ and not by the works of the law; for by the works of the law no flesh will be justified"* (Gal. 2:16).

Paul continues to say to Peter, "Don't you know that neither circumcision nor any other law can justify us, so how can it justify the Gentiles? The law will not justify anyone! Only by faith in Jesus Christ, who fulfilled the law for us, can one be justified."

> *"But if, while we seek to be justified by Christ, we ourselves also are found sinners, is therefore Christ the minister of sin? God forbid"* (Gal. 2:17, KJV).

Paul is still talking to Peter and telling him we must be justified by faith in Christ. When we sin, because we will from time to time until one day we are glorified, it does not mean that Christ is condoning sin. God forbid! Jesus Christ and Him crucified is the only answer for sin.

> *"For if I build again those things which I destroyed, I make myself a transgressor"* (Gal. 2:18).

To understand what Paul was saying regarding what he had destroyed, we must refer to Philippians 3:3-9. What was destroyed was confidence in the flesh (circumcised the eighth day, of the tribe of Benjamin, a Pharisee, zealous, righteousness which is in the law, blameless). However, Paul goes on to say in verse 8, that he counted all those things as worthless, that he may gain Christ.

What Paul is telling Peter here in Galatians 2:18 is that if he goes back to what he destroyed, he would be leaving the new covenant. If we go back to faith in the law, we will come out from under the new covenant, which will make us a transgressor! A transgressor of both the law that we cannot keep and the new covenant, which is deliverance from the law!

Can you see here the deceitful heart of man? Even the apostle Peter is attempting to put men back under law for justification. Sadly, we all have this bent in us that continues to try and justify ourselves by law. Any law. When we go back to law, we are saying that the blood of Jesus is not enough! What is law, you ask? Anything and everything that is not faith in Jesus Christ and Him crucified!

> "For I through the law died to the law that I might live to God" (Gal. 2:19).

"Peter, I needed to die! The law said do this, and I knew that the law was good, but I could not do it" (Rom. 7). "Peter, the law killed me, and it was a good death, a death to self-effort, a death to the law! Peter, the law did not die, I died to the law—there is a big difference."

> *"Knowing this: that the law is not made for a righteous person, but for the lawless and insubordinate, for the ungodly and for sinners"* (I Tim. 1:9).

The law of God will never die, it is eternal and unchanging. However, the Ten Commandments are for the unredeemed. When we came to God by faith in Jesus Christ and His finished work of the cross, we were justified and made righteous by Jesus' death on the cross (Rom. 5:19). The law was fulfilled in Christ. The law has done its job, and now we are dead to the law. Our relationship with the law has been broken. We are to live under grace and not under law.

> *"I am crucified with Christ: nevertheless I live; yet not I, but Christ liveth in me: and the life which I now live in the flesh I live by the faith of the Son of God, who loved me and gave Himself for me"* (Gal. 2:20, KJV).

With our faith now in Jesus and His shed blood, God sees us in Christ on the cross. It is the law of the Spirit of life in Christ Jesus (Rom. 8:2).

"Peter, please listen to me; I have been crucified with Christ! And Peter, that law of the Holy Spirit has made me free from the law of sin and death! It is no longer I who live, but Christ lives in me."

Glory to His name! I am in Him and He is in me! Of course I am still in this flesh, but I am living by the faith of the Son of God! That faith must be the faith of the Son of God. Not faith in a law, or faith in my faith, or being a Jew, or anything else. It is only by the faith of the Son of God! Jesus loved us so much that He went to the cross! His faith never failed! That is the only object of faith that the Father is pleased with. God loved us so much that He gave (on the cross) His only begotten Son (John 3:16).

> *"I do not frustrate the grace of God: for if righteousness come by the law, then Christ is dead in vain"* (Gal. 2:21, KJV)

The apostle Paul finishes his recount of his confrontation with Peter by saying, *"I do not frustrate* [set aside] *the grace of God: for if righteousness come by the law, then Christ died in vain."*

The Holy Spirit through Paul tells Peter, and you and I today, that we must understand that the cross satisfied all the demands of the law. Christ fulfilled the law by never sinning and then shedding His own blood on the cross. The cross is the ultimate expression of God's grace! For by grace we have been saved, and that grace is the blood shed by Jesus on the cross.

Through faith in the finished work of Jesus, we have been delivered from the demands of the law. If we look to anything other than the cross of Christ, we have gone back to law. We have set aside the grace of God, and we must not do this. We are then frustrating the grace of God and making the cross of Christ of none effect in our lives (I Cor. 1:17).

In the following verse, the Holy Spirit has Paul turn his attention to the church as a whole.

> *"O foolish Galatians! Who has bewitched you that you should not obey the truth, before whose eyes Jesus Christ was clearly portrayed among you as crucified?"* (Gal. 3:1).

The Holy Spirit, through the apostle Paul, now asks the churches in Galatia, and the church today, "Who has bewitched you?" Someone had bewitched the churches of Galatia, who had previously and clearly seen Jesus Christ crucified. They had known that the cross is where their faith was to remain.

The word *bewitched* in the Greek is *baskno,* meaning "to look at with an envious evil eye." So who is envious of you and wants to enslave you with a man-made system? Who came and told you to look to something other than the cross? Who wrote that book you are reading that tells you to follow a system of man to learn how to live for God? Brothers and sisters, don't you know that is law?

When the Christian gets deceived into attempting to live for God by any other means than by faith in the cross of Christ, they become slaves to that thing. A perfect example today, as I write this, is the G12 system. It is not biblical!

The founder does not claim it is biblical. He admits it came to him or his wife in a dream. A dream from God will always line up with the Word of God. But all over the world men and women of God are being enslaved to this different gospel. They are leaving the truth of Jesus Christ and Him crucified.

I was invited to preach for a pastor in the Philippines, and I saw on his bulletin board this false way of living for God, the G12 system. I challenged him with the truth of the Word of God that says we are to go and make disciples or followers of Christ; not, "every believer is a leader." He broke down in disgrace and told me if he doesn't follow this program, then his denomination will take away his home and the church that he had founded and built up for the last twenty years.

Instead of making disciples, followers of Jesus, this G12 system lifts up the pride of man ("I can be a leader!"). It is nothing more than a money-grabbing, church growth method that enslaves its followers. God has a church growth plan. It is called the five-fold ministry (Eph. 4:11).

We are not to be bewitched into trying some plan of a poor pathetic man. God has provided all we need by sending His Son to die on the cross.

> *"This only I want to learn from you: Did you receive the Spirit by the works of the law, or by the hearing of faith? Are you so foolish? Having begun in the Spirit, are you now being made perfect by the flesh?"* (Gal. 3:2-3).

Once again, let it be understood that anything that is not faith in Jesus Christ and Him crucified becomes a law. And our flesh loves to perform laws to try and please God. Faith in the cross is the only thing that gives the Holy Spirit the legal right to move in the life of a Christian.

> Faith versus law.
> The cross versus programs of man.
> God's wisdom versus man's wisdom.
> Spirit versus flesh.

Notice the exact words in Galatians 3:3, *"being made perfect."* This is talking about the sanctification process that we are trying to teach in this book. How foolish we Christians have become when we fall for a program of man instead of simple faith in Jesus Christ and his finished work of the cross. It is the progressive sanctification process, being made holy and set apart that all believers are in. The programs of man, laws, will never make us perfect. But when our faith remains in the sacrifice of God's Son, we are perfect in His eyes! Glory to God!

How to live for God in plain language:
"I have been crucified with Christ!"

HOW TO LIVE FOR GOD
in plain language...

CHAPTER 24

JUSTIFICATION BY FAITH

CHAPTER TWENTY-FOUR

JUSTIFICATION BY FAITH

The more I travel and teach pastor conferences, I am continuously amazed at the lack of understanding of justification in the church. In this chapter, we will look at the Bible in the hope that all born-again believers will come to know who they are in Christ. We are forgiven, saved, delivered from our sin, and adopted into the family of God. It is not by what we have done, or even what we will do or not do in the future, but by simple faith in what Jesus did for us on the cross!

The word *justified* in the Greek is *dikaioo*, meaning "to justify; the act which declares a person just and righteous in the sight of God." However, the definition does not stop simply at not guilty, or even innocent of all charges. It actually means "just as if I never sinned." Wow! This depth of love, grace, and mercy of our thrice-holy God is beyond our carnal minds to begin to understand.

> "Now we know that whatever the law says, it says to those who are under the law, that every mouth may be stopped, and all the world may become guilty before God" (Rom. 3:19).

The Bible is talking here about the Ten Commandments. It was given to stop the mouth of every person on the face of the earth and show us all that we are guilty before God. What could we possibly say in the courtroom of heaven when the Judge, God the Father, asks us how we plead regarding our sin? Our mouths will be stopped because God's commandments said, *"Thou shalt not bear false witness,"* but we all have lied. *"Thou shalt not steal,"* but we have all stolen something in our lives. The law shows that the whole world is guilty before God, and the law shuts our mouths, leaving us with nothing to argue about before a holy God.

> *"Therefore by the deeds of the law no flesh will be justified in His sight, for by the law is the knowledge of sin"* (Rom. 3:20)

No law, not even the law of God given on Mount Sinai, can justify our sin. The law was not given by God to justify us but to show us that we were sinners and out of His covenant. By the law is the knowledge of sin. We can think about the law as a mirror. We look in the mirror and see dirt on our face. It has revealed the problem, but we cannot clean our face with the mirror. The law shows us our problem of sin but there is no power in the law to take away sin. The law brought us to Jesus.

What is law? Anything and everything we put our faith in that is not Jesus Christ and Him crucified becomes a law. If our faith is not in the cross of Christ, it is a law. If we use the law improperly and try to justify ourselves by keeping a law, we will become a miserable, defeated Christian.

We cannot keep the law; God knew that when He gave the law. He did not give the law to justify us but to show us that the problem was our sin. The law is for the ungodly and sinners, not for the righteous (I Tim. 1:9). Jesus fulfilled the law for us!

> *"But now the righteousness of God apart from the law is revealed, being witnessed by the Law and the Prophets"* (Rom. 3:21).

We will never be righteous before a holy God by any law. With our faith only in the cross of Christ, we have the righteousness of Jesus imputed or credited unto us. We are righteous apart from the law! We are righteous in the sight of God by faith in Christ's finished work of the cross. Thank You, Father, for our justification by faith alone!

Romans 3:21 here tells us that all the law and all the prophets witnessed to the righteousness of God. What is the righteousness of God that all the law and all the prophets revealed? On the Mount of Transfiguration we see exactly what the righteousness of God is.

> *"Now it came to pass, about eight days after these sayings, that He took Peter, John, and James and went up on the mountain to pray. As He prayed, the appearance of His face was altered, and His robe became white and glistening"* (Luke 9:28-29).

Jesus Himself took the three disciples up on the mountain to pray. When the disciples looked at Jesus, He was white and glistening. Wow! Think about this incredible moment for Peter, James, and John. What they would see and hear that day!

> *"And behold, two men talked with Him, who were Moses and Elijah"* (Luke 9:30).

Then, all of a sudden, they saw Moses and Elijah talking with Jesus! Moses, who represented the law; and Elijah, who represented the prophets! All the law and all the prophets point to the righteousness of God.

What do you think Moses and Elijah were talking with Jesus about? Do you think Moses was talking to Jesus about the giving of the law on Mount Sinai, or Elijah was talking about being translated into heaven in a chariot of fire? No! All the law and all the prophets witness to the righteousness of God (Rom. 3:21). What is the righteousness of God?

CHAPTER TWENTY-FOUR JUSTIFICATION BY FAITH | 247

> *"Who appeared in glory and spoke of His decease which He was about to accomplish at Jerusalem"* (Luke 9:31).

They were talking about Jesus going to the cross! They were talking about the righteousness of God, which is Jesus Christ and Him crucified! The cross is where and how we are made righteous. The cross is where and how we are justified in the sight of a holy God.

Notice what the Word of God says, *"He was about to accomplish at Jerusalem."* No man took His life! He gave it freely for you and for me. He came to die on the cross to make us righteous. This is what all the law and all the prophets witnessed to! It was the greatest accomplishment the world will ever see.

Romans 3:21 continues to say the righteousness of God is apart from any law. The only way we can be righteous before a holy God is to put our faith exclusively in the cross of Christ. Not law! Not even God's Ten commandments or God's ceremonial law. Not a law of man! Not a law we make for ourselves! When we make a law out of a good Christian discipline like Bible reading or prayer to try and justify ourselves before God, it will have the opposite effect. We will be guilty of moving our faith off of the sacrifice of God's Son that the law was designed to point us to.

> *"Even the righteousness of God, through faith in Jesus Christ, to all and on all who believe. For there is no*

difference; for all have sinned and fall short of the glory of God" (Rom. 3:22-23).

We are righteous by keeping our faith in the sacrifice of God's Son and only in the finished work of the cross. How wonderful! How simple! Yes, but not that easy for Christians to do. Our default position is to try and please God by what we do instead of by simple faith in what Jesus has already done on the cross.

This verse goes on to say that the righteousness of God is the same for all that believe. There is no difference. Let us compare a pastor who has been saved thirty-five years to a young girl, twelve years old, who was saved last week. The pastor has seen hundreds of people come to Christ under his ministry, has planted churches, and has been used of God in a powerful way. The young girl who got saved last week has done nothing yet to advance the kingdom of God. She has not even read the Bible.

Who is more righteous? Who is more justified in the sight of God? Neither! There is no difference; they are the same! They are both justified and have the righteousness of God by putting their faith in Jesus Christ and Him crucified. It is not what the pastor has done that justifies him. They are the same because *"all have sinned and fall short of the glory of God."* Sin is the problem, and faith in the blood of Jesus is the only way that anyone can be justified, declared not guilty!

CHAPTER TWENTY-FOUR JUSTIFICATION BY FAITH

> *"Being justified freely by His grace through the redemption that is in Christ Jesus"* (Rom. 3:24).

This is our position—justified! It's free! By His grace we are redeemed and brought back into relationship with the Father through faith in the sacrifice of His Son. We do not deserve this position and we cannot earn justification. This is a decree from God—justified! It is a verdict! The verdict of not guilty! We are declared justified by God because of our faith in the sacrifice of His only begotten Son!

It is very important for the Christian to understand that we do not lose our position of justified every time we sin. As long as our faith is in the cross of Jesus, we are justified. Our daily condition will not equal our position until the day we are glorified, but we are still justified even when we commit a sin.

This is hard for many Christians to believe because we do not understand that the cross of Christ was a legal work. This is God's plan. The only way to make us acceptable to Him is when our faith remains in that plan alone. We are justified, just as if we never sinned!

> *"For it pleased the Father that in Him all the fullness should dwell. And by Him to reconcile all things to Himself, by Him, whether things on earth or things in heaven, having made peace through the blood of His cross"* (Col. 1:19-20).

Everything is in Christ! Jesus pleased the Father. That is where the Christian needs to dwell—in Christ. How? Through the blood of the cross. From Genesis to Revelation the Bible points to the blood.

That is where our peace with the Father comes from—the cross! The struggling Christian who does not have peace is not resting in the finished work of Jesus.

> *"And you, who once were alienated and enemies in your mind by wicked works, yet now He has reconciled"* (Col. 1:21).

Before we were justified, we were alienated and enemies of God. You might say, "No, I wasn't an enemy of God!" The Bible says we all were. But now we are washed in the blood of the cross and are no longer enemies of God. We have now been reconciled. How did Jesus do this? Through the body of his flesh on the cross! That is why Jesus came as a man, so He could shed His blood and die for us all.

> *"In the body of His flesh, through death, to present you holy, and blameless, and above reproach in His sight"* (Col. 1:22).

Now, with our faith in the blood of His cross, Jesus presents us holy, blameless, and above reproach to God! Wow, what a decree! We are holy in the sight of a thrice-holy God!

When we sin, because we are still not perfect, *"we have an Advocate with the Father, Jesus Christ the righteous"* (I John 2:1).

I can hear some of you now, "Are you saying that we can just go ahead and sin?" Don't think like that! No, of course not! God will never condone sin! The Bible does not teach unconditional eternal security. That is man trying to justify his sin (Gal. 5:21). We cannot practice sin and get away with it.

There is a condition. Let us look at the condition of being holy, blameless, and above reproach in the sight of God. Go to the next verse. *"If…."*

> *"If indeed you continue in the faith, grounded and steadfast, and are not moved away from the hope of the gospel which you heard"* (Col. 1:23).

You are holy, blameless, and above reproach in His sight, *"If indeed you continue in the faith!"* Not if you don't sin, or not if you go to church, not by praying and fasting. No, not by your works lest any man should boast (Eph. 2:9). You are holy, blameless, and above reproach in the sight of God by faith alone!

As long as you keep your faith in the cross of Christ, you have peace with the Father through the blood of His Son. Don't move away! Stay grounded and be steadfast in the hope of the gospel. Be honest and believe the Word of God. You can lose your justification if you stop believing.

This verse is only one of many that teaches us that there is an "if."

"How shall we escape if we neglect so great a salvation" (Heb. 2:3). Yes, you can lose your salvation if you stop believing. Sadly, I have known a number of brethren that have lost their way and no longer believe.

But if we continue in the faith, then we are holy, blameless, and above reproach in the sight of God! We are justified by faith in the finished work of Jesus. Thank You, Lord, for the blood Jesus shed on the cross!

How to live for God in plain language:
Justified by continuing in the faith!

# HOW TO LIVE FOR
GOD
in plain language…

CHAPTER 25

GOD THE JUSTIFIER

CHAPTER TWENTY-FIVE
GOD THE JUSTIFIER

"Whom God set forth as a propitiation by His blood, through faith, to demonstrate His righteousness, because in His forbearance God had passed over the sins that were previously committed" (Rom. 3:25).

Sin is the problem; the blood is the answer. *"Without shedding of blood there is no remission* [of sin]*"* (Heb. 9:22). There is no justification without the shedding of the blood of Jesus. That big fancy word, *propitiation,* simply means "payment in full." Jesus paid for our righteousness with His precious blood. We have no righteousness of our own, not before we are saved and not after we are saved. It is His righteousness! God passed over our sins and declared us justified by faith in the finished work of His Son. Everything we receive from God comes by faith in the cross. Thank You, Lord, for the obedience of your Son unto death, even the death of the cross! (Phil. 2:8).

> *"To demonstrate at the present time His righteousness, that He might be just and the justifier of the one who has faith in Jesus"* (Rom. 3:26).

Once again, the Holy Spirit writes through the apostle Paul, of "His righteousness." God told Adam, "The day you eat of the Tree of the Knowledge of Good and Evil, you shall surely die" (Gen. 2:17). God must remain true to His word. He must be a just judge. He cannot deny His Word. Sin would have to be paid for in order for Him to be a just judge. Brother Swaggart says it well, "God could speak the world into existence, but He could not speak sin and death out of existence." God sent His only begotten Son to pay our sin debt that we could not pay, *"that He might be just and the justifier of the one who has faith in Jesus."* Glory to God and the Lamb forever! God is the justifier!

> *"Where is boasting then? It is excluded. By what law? Of works? No, but by the law of faith. Therefore we conclude that a man is justified by faith apart from the deeds of the law"* (Rom. 3:27-28).

Wow! God has a law called the law of faith! God's laws never change. He is not a man that He should lie (Num. 23:19). If we have our faith in the proper object, Jesus Christ and Him crucified and not our works or any other law, then we can conclude that we are justified! It is a law of God. It is the law of faith! With our faith in the cross of Christ, God has declared a verdict of not guilty, innocent of all charges, just as if we never sinned! Hallelujah! This is the kind of God we are serving!

I want us to move to the first five verses of the next chapter of Romans, so we might see, once and for all, that we are, in fact, justified by faith in the blood of the Lamb and not by anything that we do.

> *"What shall we say that Abraham our father has found according to the flesh? For if Abraham was justified by works, he has something to boast about, but not before God"* (Rom. 4:1-2).

All of our good works do not justify us before a holy God. "Nothing in my hands I bring, simply to the cross I cling!" Amen! Ask yourself, "What can I do to add to the finished work of Jesus?" Simply believe, and God will declare you not guilty! But the all-important question is, believe what? Believe in the finished work on the cross of the only begotten Son of God. Then you will have everlasting life! (John 3:16).

> *"For what does the Scripture say? 'Abraham believed God, and it was accounted to him for righteousness"* (Rom. 4:3).

What was it that Abraham believed? As always, we find the answer in the Scriptures.

> *"And the Scripture, foreseeing that God would justify the Gentiles by faith, preached the gospel to Abraham beforehand, saying, 'In you all nations shall be blessed'"* (Gal. 3:8).

The Bible here tells us that God Himself preached to Abraham! God was going to send His Son through Abraham's loins, and He would shed His blood for the sins of all mankind. That is the gospel! Abraham believed God, and it was accounted to him as righteousness. It is the same for us today, simply believe! Righteousness by faith in the sacrifice of God's Son alone!

> *"Now to him who works, the wages are not counted as grace but as debt"* (Rom. 4:4).

We are saved by grace, not of works, lest anyone should boast (Eph. 2:8-9). The Bible says here if we try to work for justification, the eternal verdict of not guilty, by even doing a good thing, we are telling God He owes us a debt. "Ok God, I read five chapters in the Bible and prayed for an hour today, so You owe me!" Yes, even good Christian disciplines can become works to try and please the Father.

I was saved for about two years. I was going to a prayer meeting every Saturday night. After going to the prayer meeting for all that time, I did not want to go anymore. I think some of you know what I am talking about. I just did not want to go every Saturday night anymore! I thought if I went to the prayer meeting, God would be pleased with me, and if I did not go, He would not be pleased with me.

> *"But without faith it is impossible to please Him, for he who comes to God must believe that He is, and that He is a rewarder of those who diligently seek Him"* (Heb. 11:6).

The Scripture says, *"Without faith it is impossible to please Him."* Faith in what? Our prayer meetings? Of course not! The prayer meeting was at 7 p.m. I would sit in my house and watch the clock while talking to God. 6:45 p.m., "Lord, I would rather stay home tonight." 6:50 p.m., "I would just like to be with my family tonight." 6:55 p.m., "Okay God, I am going to the prayer meeting!" Then I would get in my truck, drive to the church, and pray for thirty or forty minutes.

On the way home, I would talk to the Lord. "I went to the prayer meeting. You saw me there, give me my points; give me my gold star. I am more holy now. Oh, and by the way, Lord, I did not see Brother Steve there tonight. I don't think he was there last week either." Self-righteousness! I had created my own law. By going to the prayer meeting, I was trying to please Him and make myself righteous. Our faith must be in the sacrifice of His Son. If our faith is in anything we are doing, we are telling God He owes us.

> *"But we are all like an unclean thing, and all our righteousnesses are like filthy rags"* (Isa. 64:6).

In the Hebrew language, the filthy rags in this verse refer to a woman's menstrual cloth. When we present to God what we are doing to try to please Him, even a good thing like a prayer meeting, we are offering up that filthy, dirty blood instead of the pure, clean, precious blood of Jesus! I learned that I had made a law out of going to the prayer meetings. I was trying to please God and make myself righteous. Now, I go to prayer meetings to spend time with Him and get direction in my life, not to please Him, but because I love the Lord.

Are you trying to please God by what you do? Or will you simply please God by faith in what Jesus already did for you on the cross? I had to repent of placing my faith in going to the prayer meetings. "Oh Lord, forgive me for looking to what I do instead of what Jesus did for me on the cross!" Freedom came the day I took my faith off myself and put it back where it belonged—on Jesus Christ and Him crucified! We must stop any effort of our own to please God or to gain victory over sin.

> *"But to him who does not work but believes on Him who justifies the ungodly, his faith is accounted for righteousness"* (Rom. 4:5).

We must simply believe, and then our faith will be accounted for righteousness. Do not be confused by this Scripture! It is not saying that we do not work for the Lord. It is saying we cannot work for righteousness. Of course we do what He asks us to do! It is our blessing to serve Him. But we cannot add to the finished work of the cross! We only believe on Him! Not in a church system, a denominational rule, or our works. Only believe on Jesus and His finished work of the cross, and we are justified.

How to live for God in plain language:
Just as if I never sinned! Glory to God and the Lamb slain before the foundation of the world!

HOW TO LIVE FOR GOD
in plain language...

CHAPTER 26

SALVATION OF THE SINNER

CHAPTER TWENTY-SIX

SALVATION OF THE SINNER

"*For all have sinned and fall short of the glory of God*" (Rom. 3:23).

"*For the wages of sin is death, but the gift of God is eternal life in Jesus Christ our Lord*" (Rom. 6:23).

We are all born sinners, born with sin, separated from God by our sin, and we all deserve death. The world does not like to talk about sin, and the church world is trying to ignore sin. But the Word of God mentions sin more than a hundred times in the New Testament alone!

"*But your iniquities have separated you from your God;
And your sins have hidden His face from you*" (Isa. 59:2).

God shows in His Word that sin is the problem, and the only answer for sin is the sacrifice of His only begotten Son.

Adam sinned in the garden, and sin passed to all men. Adam's children were born sinners, their children were born sinners, their children were sinners, all the way down to us. We are born sinners. We do not sin and become a sinner; we are born sinners, and that is why we sin.

> "But He was wounded for our transgressions, He was bruised for our iniquities; The chastisement for our peace was upon Him ... And the Lord has laid on Him the iniquity of us all" (Isa. 53:5, 6).

> "But God demonstrates His own love toward us, in that while we were still sinners, Christ died for us" (Rom. 5:8).

> "I am the good shepherd. The good shepherd gives His life for the sheep" (John 10:11).

> "For by grace you have been saved through faith, and that not of yourselves; it is the gift of God, not of works, lest anyone should boast" (Eph. 2:8-9).

> "In whom we have redemption through His blood, the forgiveness of sins" (Col. 1:14).

> "And the blood of Jesus Christ His Son cleanses us from all sin" (I John 1:7).

CHAPTER TWENTY-SIX **SALVATION OF THE SINNER** | **267**

Jesus was not born of a man. If Jesus would have been born of an earthly father, He would have also been born a sinner. But the Holy Spirit came upon the virgin, and she did conceive, so Jesus was born without sin (Luke 1:35). He would be the perfect sacrifice to pay for our sin.

The Bible says, *"For God so loved the world that He gave His only begotten Son, that whoever believes in Him should not perish but have everlasting life"* (John 3:16).

> *"But as many as received Him, to them He gave the right to become children of God, to those who believe in His name: who were born, not of blood, nor of the will of the flesh, nor of the will of man, but of God"* (John 1:12-13).

Jesus said, *"Most assuredly, I say to you, unless one is born again, he cannot see the kingdom of God"* (John 3:3).

Jesus said, *"That which is born of the flesh is flesh, and that which is born of the Spirit is spirit. Do not marvel that I said to you, 'You must be born again.' The wind blows where it wishes, and you hear the sound of it, but cannot tell where it comes from and where it goes. So is everyone who is born of the Spirit"* (John 3:6-8).

Being a good person cannot pay for our sin. Being born in a Christian home does not make us a Christian. Even going to church does not take away our sin. We must be born again of the Spirit!

When Adam rebelled in the garden and ate of the Tree of the Knowledge of Good and Evil, sin entered the world, and the Holy Spirit had to leave Adam. He died spiritually. Adam's sin caused separation from God. God will not have sin in His presence.

That is why Jesus said we must be born again of the Spirit! We are born without the Spirit of God in us. When the repentant sinner asks God to forgive him of his sins and confesses Jesus as his Lord and Savior, the Holy Spirit comes into his heart and life. He is born again! A spiritual rebirth! Glory to God and the Lamb forever!

But wait a minute! What about a murderer? The Bible says, liars and murderers will have their place in the lake of fire (Rev. 21:8). God makes no distinction between sins. Moses killed two Egyptians, and he is in heaven today. King David committed adultery and murder, and he also is in heaven. They repented of their sin and put their faith in the Messiah to come that would shed His blood for their sins.

> "*Without shedding of blood there is no remission* [of sin]" (Heb. 9:22).

> "'*Come now, and let us reason together,*' *says the Lord, 'Though your sins are like scarlet, they shall be as white as snow; Though they are red like crimson, they shall be as wool'*" (Isa. 1:18).

> "*He who believes in Him is not condemned; but he who does not believe is condemned already, because he has not*

believed in the name of the only begotten Son of God. And this is the condemnation, that the light has come into the world, and men loved darkness rather than light, because their deeds were evil" (John 3:18-19).

We will all be judged, not by man or a religious system, but by the Word of God.

Jesus said, *"I am the way, the truth, and the life. No one comes to the Father except through Me"* (John 14:6).

> *"And it is appointed for men to die once, but after this the judgment"* (Heb. 9:27).

There is no opportunity after we die! The false teaching of purgatory has sent millions to hell because one is taught that they will have the opportunity to atone for their sins after they die. No! That is a lie from the pit of hell! Purgatory is not in the Bible!

> *"Behold, now is the accepted time; behold, now is the day of salvation"* (II Cor. 6:2).

If you are reading this book and are not sure of your eternal destiny, do not wait to make that decision! When we are born of our mother, we have a birthday, a moment in time. The date and time of our birth is recorded in the hospital and put on our birth certificate. There are witnesses to our birth.

When you are born again, like Jesus said we must be to enter into heaven, it is the same. It is a moment in time. You may not know the exact date, but you will never forget the place and the moment you received Christ as your Lord and Savior!

If you are reading this, and you do not know where you were when the Lord saved you, and you are not sure that you will go to heaven when you die, and you want to be born again, I want to pray with you right now! Saying a prayer does not save you, but if you believe what you are praying with all of your heart, then your sins will be washed in the blood of the Lamb in an instant!

You are talking directly to the Father. Let us pray:

> "Dear God in heaven, I come to You in the name of Your Son, Jesus. I am sorry for my sins and the way I have lived. Please forgive me. I believe that Jesus is Your Son, and I believe that He died on the cross to pay for my sins. Wash me with His precious blood and cleanse me from all my sins. With my mouth, I confess that Jesus Christ is Your Son and that He died on the cross and rose from the dead. Right now, I take my faith off religion, off myself, and I put my faith only on the sacrifice of Your Son on the cross. I receive Jesus as my Lord and Savior! According to Your Word, the Bible, my sins are gone, and I am saved! I will live for You all the days of my life! Thank You, Father! Thank You for Jesus! Let the Holy Spirit lead my life. Amen!"

Glory to God! You are now a born-again Christian and on your way to heaven. Praise the Lord! Burdens are lifted at Calvary!

> *"These things I have written to you who believe in the name of the Son of God, that you may know that you have eternal life, and that you may continue to believe in the name of the Son of God"* (I John 5:13).

Now the Holy Spirit lives in you, and you know that you know that your sins are forgiven, and you are on your way to heaven! Thank You, Lord, for the simplicity that is the gospel. Hallelujah!

Call a Christian friend or relative and tell them of your decision. They will be very happy for you. Read and believe the Bible.

Please contact us at It is Finished Ministries and let us know of this wonderful decision. May the Lord bless you!

HOW TO LIVE FOR GOD

in plain language...

CHAPTER 27

BAPTIZED INTO THE HOLY SPIRIT

CHAPTER TWENTY-SEVEN
BAPTIZED INTO THE HOLY SPIRIT

The word *baptism* in the Greek is *baptizo,* and it simply means "to be immersed or submerged, to saturate." The Bible speaks of different types of baptisms. We will review a few before we learn of the baptism in the Holy Spirit.

> "Or do you not know that as many of us as were baptized into Christ Jesus were baptized into His death" (Rom. 6:3).

From this verse, we see that we must be baptized into Christ's death while He was on the cross to be free from the penalty of sin. When we first believed and received Christ, we were immersed into His death on the cross. Our old man was crucified with Christ (Rom. 6:3, Gal. 2:20, Eph. 2:4-6).

WATER BAPTISM

> "When He had been baptized, Jesus came up immediately from the water; and behold, the heavens were opened to

> Him, and He saw the Spirit of God descending like a dove and alighting upon Him" (Matt. 3:16).

> "Now as they went down the road, they came to some water. And the eunuch said, 'See, here is water. What hinders me from being baptized?' Then Philip said, 'If you believe with all your heart, you may.' And he answered and said, 'I believe that Jesus Christ is the Son of God.' So he commanded the chariot to stand still. And both Philip and the eunuch went down into the water, and he baptized him" (Acts 8:36-38).

This is the water baptism that all believers are very familiar with. Being baptized in water is an outward profession of our faith now being in the sacrifice of God's Son. After we believe, we are immersed under the water which symbolizes our death with Christ. Then, symbolizing our born-again experience, we come up from under the water, typifying Jesus' resurrection from the dead and our new life in Christ. When we receive Jesus as our Lord and Savior, the Holy Spirit comes into us. We are born again of the Spirit as Jesus said in John 3.

BAPTIZED IN THE HOLY SPIRIT

> "I indeed baptized you with water, but He will baptize you with the Holy Spirit" (Mark 1:8).

In this verse, John makes it very clear and teaches us that there is more for the believer than the initial baptism into Christ's death. More than water baptism. John the Baptist is teaching and proclaiming that Jesus will come and baptize us with the Holy Spirit.

Please, let the Lord show you, through this simple biblical teaching, that each and every believer needs the baptism in the Holy Spirit as the Bible teaches. It is a distinctively separate work of God in the life of the born-again believer. The Word of God does not change. Spiritual things are spiritually discerned. We live in a very confusing and demonic world today. We need the infilling of the Holy Spirit's power to help us stay focused on the victory that Christ has provided on the cross!

> *"And being assembled together with them, He commanded them not to depart from Jerusalem, but to wait for the Promise of the Father, 'which,' He said, 'you have heard from Me; for John truly baptized with water, but you shall be baptized with the Holy Spirit not many days from now'"* (Acts 1:4-5).

After the resurrection, Jesus was speaking with the disciples and commanded them not to depart until they had received the "Promise of the Father." This was not a suggestion by Jesus, it was a command! What was that promise? To be baptized with the Holy Spirit!

Look what Jesus said to His disciples just before He ascended into heaven.

> *"But you shall receive power when the Holy Spirit has come upon you; and you shall be witnesses to Me in Jerusalem, and in all Judea and Samaria, and to the end of the earth"* (Acts 1:8).

How much more today should we heed the words of our Lord and Savior and receive that power source, the Holy Spirit, as we step out to do what He has called us to do? Every born-again believer should want to be a witness for Christ. Many Christians have the desire to do the work of an evangelist as the Word tells us, but they do not open their mouth when opportunity presents itself for the fear of man. The Holy Spirit gives us the boldness to proclaim the gospel to a hurting and dying world. Praise the name of Jesus! Thank You, Lord, for the baptism in the Holy Spirit that helps us to be witnesses of You and for sending us the power!

I would refer to myself the first two and one-half years after salvation as a pew warmer. I was saved and going to church, growing in the grace and knowledge of Him but not a bold witness. But then, at a camp meeting, the need for the baptism in the Holy Spirit was preached. The preacher said it is a gift and all believers need this baptism. My eleven-year-old daughter went to the altar to be baptized with the Holy Spirit. When I saw her receive the infilling with the evidence of speaking with other tongues, I immediately was baptized just like Jesus promised and spoke with an unknown tongue. I was not seeking to speak in tongues. I desired that God would give me all He had for me, and this was the gift the Father promised.

What an incredible change occurred in my life after I was baptized in the Holy Spirit! My praise and worship became much deeper. A strong desire to be a witness for Christ came over me. I understood the Bible better. My prayer life increased and with more power. I began doing the work of an evangelist that I had not done previously.

With the work He has called me to do, it is all-important that the Holy Spirit guide me and teach me His ways so that I may be effective in this ministry. Without the gift of the Holy Spirit, I would not be properly equipped to fulfill His call in my life. Frankly speaking, I would not be writing this book right now.

In Scripture, there is another example of the necessity of being filled with the Holy Spirit. There arose an important ministry need in the early church. Someone would need to take care of the widows, but the disciples did not have the time to do it themselves. We read in Acts 6 of this account.

> *"Therefore brethren, seek out from among you seven men of good reputation, full of the Holy Spirit and wisdom, whom we may appoint over this business; but we will give ourselves continually to prayer and to the ministry of the word. And the saying pleased the whole multitude.*

> *And they chose Stephen, a man full of faith and the Holy Spirit, and Philip, Prochorus, Nicanor, Timon, Parmenas, and Nicolas, a proselyte from Antioch, whom they set before the apostles; and when they had prayed, they laid hands on them. Then the word of God spread, and the number of the disciples multiplied greatly in Jerusalem, and a great many of the priests were obedient to the faith. And Stephen, full of faith and power, did great wonders and signs among the people"* (Acts 6:3-8).

Please look with me at the qualifications of those who were chosen to fulfill this ministry. Notice they were to seek out from among the brethren, the born-again believer. So to be clear, being saved was not the only requirement for this important work of God. There was another distinct qualification, to be full of the Holy Spirit!

When an important work is to be done for the Lord, He will choose men full of faith and the Holy Spirit, which brings power!

I want you to consider this analogy of being baptized with the Holy Spirit. When we are saved, we are like a glass that has just been filled with water. The Holy Spirit has come into our heart and lives, and we are now God's child. But when we are baptized in the Holy Spirit, like Jesus said, it is like taking that glass of water and immersing it into a river. Before, the Holy Spirit was in us and now we are in the Holy Spirit! Glory to God! We need this power source in our lives!

CHAPTER TWENTY-SEVEN BAPTIZED INTO THE HOLY SPIRIT

> *"And it happened, while Apollos was at Corinth, that Paul, having passed through the upper regions, came to Ephesus. And finding some disciples [believers] he said to them, 'Did you receive the Holy Spirit when you believed?' So they said to him, 'We have not so much as heard whether there is a Holy Spirit.' And he said to them, 'Into what then were you baptized?' So they said, 'Into John's baptism.' Then Paul said, 'John indeed baptized with a baptism of repentance, saying to the people that they should believe on Him who would come after him, that is, on Christ Jesus.' When they heard this, they were baptized in the name of the Lord Jesus. And when Paul laid hands on them, the Holy Spirit came upon them, and they spoke with tongues and prophesied"* (Acts 19:1-6).

They were already disciples. They had already believed and been baptized in water (John's baptism). But we see that when the Holy Spirit came upon them, they spoke with tongues. Tongues is the initial evidence of the baptism in the Holy Spirit. It is a language spoken somewhere on the earth but not known to the one baptized (Acts 2:6). It is a new language that glorifies God.

> *"For with stammering lips and another tongue He will speak to this people, To whom He said, 'This is the rest with which You may cause the weary to rest,' And, 'This is the refreshing'"* (Isa. 28:11-12).

Many times, when I enter an environment that has ungodly music, especially music that I used to party to as an unbeliever, I find myself automatically praying in the Spirit. My new tongue brings refreshing and peace in the midst of a storm. When I find myself under pressure, I pray in tongues in my head. My wife will counsel pregnant women who are in labor to pray in tongues to lessen the pain. It is as real as our salvation and is totally by faith. A free gift for the child of God!

> "And these signs will follow those who believe: In My name they will cast out demons; they will speak with new tongues" (Mark 16:17).

> "And they were all filled with the Holy Spirit and began to speak with other tongues, as the Spirit gave them utterance" (Acts 2:4).

> "Cretans and Arabs—we hear them speaking in our own tongues the wonderful works of God" (Acts 2:11).

> "For they heard them speak with tongues and magnify God" (Acts 10:46).

> "For he who speaks in a tongue does not speak to men but to God, for no one understands him; however, in the spirit he speaks mysteries" (I Cor. 14:2).

> *"He who speaks in a tongue edifies himself, but he who prophesies edifies the church"* (I Cor. 14:4).
>
> *"I thank my God I speak with tongues more than you all"* (I Cor. 14:18).
>
> *"Therefore, brethren, desire earnestly to prophesy, and do not forbid to speak with tongues"* (I Cor. 14:39).
>
> *"... And you shall receive the gift of the Holy Spirit. For the promise is to you and to your children, and to all who are afar off, as many as the Lord our God will call"* (Acts 2:38-39).

So whether you have been taught that it is not for today or even that it is not of God, read and believe the Word of God, and the Lord will give this wonderful gift to you. If you are a Christian who believes the Word of God, and you know that the baptism in the Holy Spirit with the evidence of speaking with tongues is real but have not received, then ask and believe, and you will be filled!

How to live for God in plain language:

By every word that proceeds out of the mouth of God, including the command to receive power from on high and be baptized in the Holy Spirit with the evidence of speaking with other tongues.

HOW TO LIVE FOR
GOD
in plain language...

CHAPTER 28

AS YOU HAVE RECEIVED

CHAPTER TWENTY-EIGHT

AS YOU HAVE RECEIVED

In this chapter, I would like to summarize how to live for God.

The Bible has taught us that the only thing that pleases our heavenly Father is our faith in the sacrifice of His Son. We have learned that we all have a sin nature that wants to dominate our lives. We have also learned that a law, any law, is the strength of the sin nature. So anything we put our faith in other than the cross of Christ will become a law to us and put us back into bondage.

Just as the apostle Paul, we must have that wretched man moment, when we cry out, *"Who will deliver me from this body of death?"* and simply say and believe, *"I thank God— through Jesus Christ our Lord!"* (Rom. 7:24-25).

The Word of God has taught us that there is a more powerful law than the law of sin and death. It is the law of the Spirit of life in Christ Jesus. A believer needs to be in Christ in order to allow the Holy Spirit to go to work in their life.

We have learned how to walk in the Spirit by faith in the cross alone. Jesus said, "When the Spirit comes, He will glorify Me," not man.

You will now have more discernment regarding false doctrine and man's foolish ways to try and live for God because you have learned that anything that is not faith in the cross becomes a law.

> "As you therefore have received Christ Jesus the Lord, so walk in Him, rooted and built up in Him and established in the faith, as you have been taught, abounding in it with thanksgiving" (Col. 2:6-7).

This Bible verse is telling us that the same way we received Jesus, by grace through faith, is how we must walk in Him. The day we put our faith in the finished work of our Lord and Savior Jesus Christ, we were justified, just as if we never sinned! The blood was applied to our lives, and we became a new creation in Christ. So now we walk in Him, by grace through faith! This is the progressive sanctification process. *"Sanctified by faith in Me,"* Jesus said!

The faith we walk in must have the same object as the day we were saved—the blood shed on the cross. We cannot make ourselves holy, and we cannot set ourselves apart for God, by our own willpower. We must come to the end of ourselves and deny our own ability and willpower to try and live for God. When we try to progressively sanctify ourselves, it becomes law, and we frustrate the grace of God and fall from grace! Falling from grace is not sinning. Falling from grace is going back to a law to try to please the Father.

Our flesh will fight against the Spirit when we put our faith in anything other than the sacrifice of God's Son. Then the works of the flesh, which no true believer wants, will follow. We have been crucified with Christ; we no longer live, but Christ lives in us, and the life we now live in the flesh, we live by faith of the Son of God, who loved us and gave Himself for us (Gal. 2:20).

The cross, the cross, the cross! Thank You, Father, for Jesus' obedience unto death, even the death of the cross!

> *"Beware lest anyone cheat you through philosophy and empty deceit, according to the tradition of men, according to the basic principles of the world, and not according to Christ. For in Him dwells all the fullness of the Godhead bodily; and you are complete in Him, who is the head of all principality and power"* (Col. 2:8-10).

How to live for God in plain language:

Die to self-effort, crucify the flesh and its lusts, die to law, die to the sin nature. Live by faith alone! Faith in Jesus Christ and Him crucified! Are you dead yet? Die, and then live the resurrected abundant life in Christ! May the Lord richly bless you with your newfound faith in Christ alone! Rest, because it is finished!